TWELVE MONTHS AND COUNTING

a true story of love, loss, grief and hope

Andy Smith

Sold in aid of Myton Hospices,
serving Warwick, Coventry & Rugby

For more information : www.andysmithmusician.com
https://www.facebook.com/andy.smith.1675/

Cover photograph : Seaton, June 2019

First paperback edition January 2021

For Helen

'We are the ink that won't fade'

x

CONTENTS

PREFACE

I woke this morning and for the briefest second, just like every other morning, I expected to hear you breathing and see you sleeping by my side. I rolled over and tried to sleep some more, but I couldn't. You are often in my dreams, it's a poor substitute, but at least it feels like I've spent some time with you.

I hate mornings, I also hate the dark evenings - but mornings are the hardest. I hate the quiet. I talk to you to break the silence, I tell you my plans for the day. I need to have plans. I need to keep busy.

I feel guilty. I'm jealous that you've escaped the pain that you've left behind and I want to be where you are. But you fought, literally to the death, to overcome the inevitable. You lost that battle, but not through want of trying - and so yes, I feel guilty that I sometimes struggle to face the day. I'm healthy, I'm surrounded by love. But you're not here!

I often wonder how you'd have coped if the tables had been turned. I'm sure that you'd have mourned in a very private way. I doubt, (in fact I know), that you wouldn't have posted your feelings on Facebook. I'm certain that you'd have been cocooned in the same love as I have, but it would have been hard for you living in 'our' house on your own. You'd have needed a very different type of support.

When you were first diagnosed, you told me, (I can picture you standing in the kitchen), that you were glad that it was you dying and not me. I glibly told you to stop being so selfish and that you weren't going to die...

But now I know what you meant, and if I could have shielded you from anything in this world, it would've been the total devastation and desolation that losing your partner brings about.

In a perfect world, we would have lived until we were old and grey, and then, holding hands, painlessly slipped away together. Unfortunately life isn't like that. More's the pity.

But if by being the 'one that's left behind', I have protected you from unimaginable pain, loneliness and tears, then I've done what I was most happy doing - and what you always wanted me to do. I've looked after you x

FIRST AND LAST SONG

FIRST SONG

The first song I sang to Helen was Vincent (*by Don McLean*), we'd met 24 hours before. The last song I sang to Helen was also Vincent, which was a couple of hours before she died.

In November 1983 the 'on-off' five-year relationship with my girlfriend ended. I was devastated. I didn't understand why and I was broken-hearted. My parents had planned to go to Derbyshire for a few days at Christmas, and I was reluctantly dragged along. I remember checking in at the hotel and being told there would be *'Afternoon Tea'* served at four o'clock. Yippee, I could hardly contain my excitement! I'm not sure if she served me my tea and biscuits, but I certainly noticed the stunning little brunette with the beautiful eyes.

In the evening, a crowd of us went to a carol service at the local church, again, she was there, sat with a bunch of other girls who were also working the Christmas break. I couldn't take my eyes off her.

Back at the hotel, the staff were much later back than the guests, and I remember sitting talking to friends in the corridor. Eventually, a crowd of about ten of them breezed through. She stared at me, really stared....I didn't know if it was contempt or attraction and I feared the former. Had she spotted my fixation on her? Oh no!

I hoped that she would be 'waiting' our table on Christmas Day, but she didn't. In fact she wasn't even serving in our dining room. *(I subsequently discovered that she had swapped with one of the other girls because she was too embarrassed to serve me.)*

Christmas Day was a Sunday and not a lot happened, but I do remember looking for a payphone. I wanted to wish my old girlfriend a 'Happy Christmas'. Ironically, it was Helen who quietly and awkwardly told me where to find it. She blushed.

In the evening I watched a James Bond film in the TV lounge with a bunch of the younger guests, then we chatted to a few members of the staff, but the one I'd hoped would be there, wasn't.

Boxing Day consisted of a wet walk in the Derbyshire hills. In the evening there was a party in the hotel's function room. It was a party very much of its time, Barn Dances, Gay Gordon's, silly games, followed by a Disco. I was sitting with a friend and his wife. He couldn't help but notice that I was struggling to keep my eyes off the trendy little brunette, dressed in a bright red flying suit, boots, pink leg warmers - and sporting very big hair!

His subtle 'Londoner' advice was, "Cor mate, imagine what your mates would think if you took her home? Get in there boy!", or words to that effect.

It was a very long walk across the hall. It seemed like ten miles, but I went back every time a new dance was announced. She kept saying 'Yes'.

By the time the disco started and all the 'oldies' had gone to bed - I think we both knew that I no longer needed to keep going back to 'my side' of the room, so we awkwardly sat together and danced the slow songs.

I've never been good at 'chat up' lines, (and a worst dancer), but I remember telling her I'd forgotten my toothbrush....I think she took pity on me.

I told her I was self-employed. For a second, she imagined me as a builder, (but not for long). When she saw my long fingernails, she decided it was possible that I was a manicurist! But when I told her I played guitar and wrote songs, it was definitely a relief and I think I ticked a box!

I discovered that she was an art student at Manchester University. Straight away I had visions of all the boyfriends who'd eagerly be awaiting her return in January, *(by which point I would be a long-forgotten memory of a Christmas where there 'wasn't a lot of choice').* She also told me that she shared a flat with a friend, who was also called Helen. Once more I had visions of wild parties, drunken students and a plethora of good-looking over-sexed males following her round like lapdogs!

I was feeling like this after an hour of talking to her. What was happening here?

Anyway, when the disco ended, we decided we would chat 'for a bit' at the top of the stairwell - which was just outside my room - and a beautiful feature of the old building.

It soon became clear that my initial fears about Helen were unfounded. She was very, very shy. She didn't have a current boyfriend and her flat mate was a 'Born-again Christian', which meant that there was no hanky-panky going on in their part of Fallowfield.

For someone who was rubbish at chatting up girls, *(despite my cool line about an absent toothbrush),* and for someone who was frighteningly shy, we talked and talked and talked. We kissed and held hands, and it wasn't long before I realised that potentially, I had the best Christmas present ever, right here by my side. We just clicked. At 2.30 a.m. we said goodnight, kissed and went to our own rooms. I think I floated to bed that night.

Tuesday was another overcast day, a crowd of us went on a coach trip to Shatton Moor and Castleton. I spent a lot of the day thinking about Helen. I wasn't sure if the previous night was a 'one off', it seemed too good to be true and she was so out of my league.

In the evening there was a 'Tropical Fancy Dress Dinner', followed by a 'Guest's Concert'. I played guitar for a few songs and Helen was in a Hawaiian singing group with the staff *(trying desperately, but unsuccessfully to hide behind the other girls).*

I remember, during the concert, she found herself sat on the row in front of me, and although I was acknowledged, it definitely wasn't the most encouraging sign. My heart sank. I decided, (and even told my friend and his wife), that it looked like I'd blown it. Perhaps I'd talked about toothbrushes a bit too much. I really couldn't read it.

After the concert, a crowd of us commandeered the lounge, it was our last night before heading home. A few members of staff came to join us, Helen knelt on the floor by the door - about as far away from me as she could. Was she playing 'hard to get' or was she regretting our Boxing Day kisses?

Someone suggested I should bring my guitar down and we could have a sing-song. I had no choice but to walk past Helen - she grinned. I fetched my guitar and when I came back, she'd made a space on the floor next to her. She smiled her beautiful smile and said, 'Sing me a song'. I melted and sang Vincent - just to her - the 'sing-song' never happened. But *we* did.

LAST SONG

Thursday August 1st 2019, 4.00pm, Helen was admitted into Myton Hospice, which is in the grounds of University Hospital, Coventry - but a very different world.

When Helen was rushed into hospital on the twentieth of July, I knew things were grim, but I still believed that the worst-case scenario was never going to happen. God wouldn't be that cruel. Besides, we were supposed to have a 'possible five years', which was still rubbish, but miracles do happen. This was nine months.

***

Mondays were our weekly 'childminding Teddy' day *(our grandson)*, a pleasure we both enjoyed, but this time I was winging it, Helen was in hospital. It was more than twice the work on my own, but he was a beautiful distraction. We'd had a fun morning and he was perched in his high chair, munching on his lunch, I was being a silly grandad - and then I got a phone call.

'Could I get to the hospital as soon as possible?' Helen had received some bad news and was asking for me.

After contacting my son-in-law, who immediately collected Teddy, I dashed to Coventry to be met by the Ward Doctor. He told me that Helen's situation had deteriorated, blood clots had moved to her lungs, and although they were doing everything possible to make her comfortable - she was dying. I went into her curtained off bay and held her – very tight.

I wanted to kill (and still do), the person who gave her the bad news. Totally alone, totally off a clipboard, totally unnecessary and totally cruel. Helen had rarely cried through the whole nightmare - but she cried that afternoon - we both did.

The following day, we were told that she needed to say goodbye to the people who were special to her. It was suggested that visits were kept to close family, because

'By Friday, she'll probably no longer be lucid'.....Friday? This is my wife. Were they telling me that by the end of the week she wouldn't even know I was there?

Our son, Ben, bravely had a conversation with her about her final wishes. She talked rationally about hymns, songs and venues. She said that she wanted to be buried somewhere near home, and have her funeral at the church where Ben and Jess had attended Rainbows, Beavers and Youth Club. How could she do that? She had a courage and strength which I was sadly lacking, both then and now.

I can't say that she gave up, because she never would, she loved life and us too much, but she must have realised that the odds were stacked very much against her.

If there was nothing more they could do to save her - I wanted her to come home. When the ambulance had driven away nearly a fortnight previously, it had never occurred to me that she wouldn't sleep in our house again. I was told that they would look into the possibility.

On the Wednesday afternoon, there was a very painful conversation with the Macmillan's nurse. She desperately tried to convince me that 'taking her home' wasn't a good idea. She suggested that they might be able to find her a bed in the hospice. She brought brochures.

I couldn't help thinking that hospices were for the dying. I still hadn't and wouldn't accept the inevitable. Helen was consulted - it had to be her decision - she wanted to go to the hospice - and so she did.

(I now know that hospices are also for the living. I still receive regular phone calls and emails from Myton, checking how we are coping – absolutely amazing!)

She wasn't expected to last the night and so the three of us stayed with her, taking shifts for an hour of unsettled sleep.

On the Friday morning, the sun was shining and her bed and oxygen tanks were wheeled into the garden. She was brought a gin and tonic, had a full body massage and watched the grandchildren playing on the lawn. It was beautifully surreal. In the afternoon, she had more visits from people who needed to say 'Goodbye'.

As the day progressed, she became notably weaker and I sensed that she was preparing to leave us. We spent another night by her bedside – my fourth night. We talked about holidays, family, friends, weddings, she sometimes opened her eyes. Frequently we'd buzz for more pain relief when we thought she was suffering. We didn't know if she was listening, but we hoped that she was.

Another night passed and she clung to life like there was no tomorrow, which was literally true. Saturday morning was very bleak, and watching her suffer was the most painful thing I've ever experienced in my life. Sometimes the drugs lasted several hours, other times their easing effect was short lived. Helen would say she was fine – when she obviously wasn't.

After a particularly distressing and upsetting episode, I was left alone in the ward with Helen and her nurse.

The day before, my son in law had kindly brought his guitar to the hospice – he thought I might appreciate having a six string friend there. It was propped against the wall where he'd left it. Unplayed.

The nurse suggested that after she'd made Helen comfortable, I might like to 'strum her a tune'. She was quietly sleeping after her last dose of painkillers. I picked up the guitar, tuned it, and sang Vincent.

By the last verse, I was a blubbering wreck. Tearfully I said, 'That was the first song I sang to you - and then we fell in love...' She opened her eyes and looked at me. I can't remember if she smiled, I just knew she'd heard me. Hopefully that meant she'd been listening to all our night time conversations. I pray that she was feeling safe in the knowledge that she was surrounded by people who loved her more than anything in this world - her family. A couple of hours later she left. She was fifty six years old. An enormous part of me died with her.

When I returned to gigging six weeks later, I avoided singing the song which was rarely off my set list. But now it's back, and if it's the 'right audience', I explain why it's so important to me. I still can't, *(and probably never will),* make it from intro to last note without thinking of our start and end.

Our first ... our last song.

Andy Smith is with **Helen Smith**.
22 December 2019 ·

Today I read the final letters of our 30 month long-distance courtship - which started after our first meeting Christmas 1983 and finished the week before our wedding in June 1986.
They have taken 20 weeks to read.
There are over 100 letters (plus a few cards) and I feel very fortunate that I have something so tangible to hang on to.
If nothing else, they are a photograph of an age before mobile phones, emails and social media.
Nobody writes letters any more – but I have a box full of envelopes with handwritten memories, silly pictures and messages of love.
On many occasions I've laughed out loud whilst reading them – Helen was very funny – I've also cried a few times – she wrote as she spoke!
Occasionally she was mad with me, (often I don't know why...and never will), but it never lasted – and by the next letter I was forgiven and regained my 'best fiancee' status!
In a few days time it will be 36 years since I first saw her captivating smile.
Life was never the same again – and despite the winter chill in Derbyshire – the sun came out in my life – and I knew that I had met my Soulmate.
Christmas was always our 'Anniversary' and so this year and every subsequent year, it is going to be hard. We will have a nice time – and the grandchildren will be a strength, (a strength which they won't be aware of), but they will make us laugh – and we will make new memories that Helen would have loved.
As for the letters – they are one of my most treasured possessions – and I will probably start reading them all over again!
No apologies for posting my first photo of Helen. This was taken the night after we 'clicked' – December 27th 1983.
Happy Christmas Babe x

PUT IT DOWN IN WRITING

We are a family of avid readers. I remember as a child thinking how wonderful it must be to write a book. I love writing lyrics and music, but a song lasts for three minutes, an average book is sixty thousand words long. How do you write something so big? What could motivate me to devote so many hours, days, weeks, months to such a project? Anyway, who would want to read it?

I've read several books on grief since Helen died – and like with the counselling I received, they have been a great help. Unfortunately, no two people's grief is the same, and so whilst there are often passages you can relate to, some of the emotions and human reactions, there are always going to be feelings which are unique to the individual.

The book I found most helpful was written by a lady called Sasha Bates (*Languages of Loss*). Sasha's husband died very suddenly – and her world fell apart. We had a connection. Sasha is a psychotherapist and had spent a large part of her working life helping the bereaved, but losing her partner made her more aware of the different nightmares and conflicting emotions that every grieving person has to swim through. There is no template.

During my counselling sessions, I was advised that writing down my feelings might be beneficial in my grieving process. In truth, it was. Just putting my raw emotions down on paper was often a cleansing experience – in the same way that a good cry can make you feel better. Often the two went hand in hand – the words and the tears.

The pain, the good days, the bad days, the anger, the total confusion, it all went down. Sometimes I would read my diatribes later and delete them – they'd served their purpose. Often I would post them on my Facebook page, not because I was looking for sympathy, *(I don't know what I was looking for),* but more as a justification, and sometimes an apology, for the weird ways I sometimes acted since losing Helen. Usually they were just a voice crying out in the darkness.

Most 'anniversaries' I would post a few paragraphs. The first month, her birthday, Christmas, New Year, my birthday, our wedding anniversary. Sometimes I'd include photos or a song that I'd written.

After twelve months had passed since Helen's death, I decided that it was probably the time to stop. I was concerned that people would be tired of my 'heart on sleeve' posts - and although I got beautiful, kind comments, I had a sneaking feeling that there might be a consensus of opinion that I needed to 'get over it'.

To say I was surprised by the reaction when I told a few friends would be an understatement. I'd failed to realise that my posts were 'appreciated' and sometimes inspirational to those who had been, or were in a similar place to me. Besides, like they said, if you didn't want to read them, you could scroll past!

I started ploughing through the last twelve months, starting with a surprisingly positive post the week before she died, to the most recent. I half expected to be embarrassed by my outpourings – but I wasn't. I felt proud that I'd had the courage to be so honest. It wasn't so much of a diary, but *(I hate the word)*, it was my journey, a journey which I now realise has no end, in fact it has only just started.

***

I'd finished 'Languages of Loss' and it occurred to me that a selection of my posts, with narrative, had the makings of a 'Grief Book'. I'm not an expert, but my knowledge is 'first hand'. I've been there, I'm *still* there. I have some idea of what it's like to lose the most important person in your whole being.

I'm very aware of the endless hours of total isolation. The notion that nobody can understand how you feel – and no one can help. The unimaginable loneliness. The tunnel without a light at the end.

The truth is, no one can understand. It's not their grief. It wasn't their partner, parent, child or friend. But regretfully, at some point in life, this trauma is going to happen to most of us. Because trauma it is.

I know that there are lost, lonely, desperately sad people out there, who are going through something similar to what I'm going through. Not the same, but similar. There are parallels. I'm writing this book because I want to help both them – and myself.

So this is my story....our story of the last fifteen months.

My surprisingly positive FACEBOOK post
26th July 2019 (one week before she died)

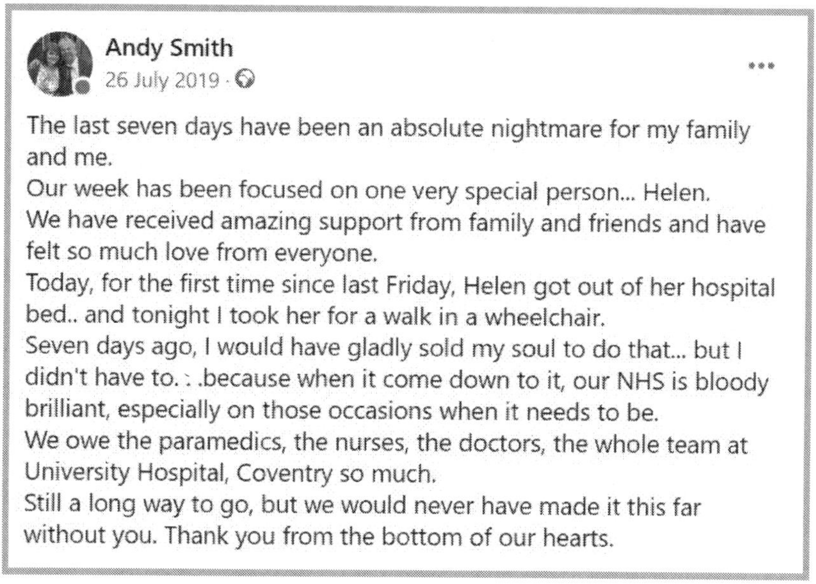
Andy Smith
26 July 2019 ·

The last seven days have been an absolute nightmare for my family and me.
Our week has been focused on one very special person... Helen.
We have received amazing support from family and friends and have felt so much love from everyone.
Today, for the first time since last Friday, Helen got out of her hospital bed.. and tonight I took her for a walk in a wheelchair.
Seven days ago, I would have gladly sold my soul to do that... but I didn't have to. : .because when it come down to it, our NHS is bloody brilliant, especially on those occasions when it needs to be.
We owe the paramedics, the nurses, the doctors, the whole team at University Hospital, Coventry so much.
Still a long way to go, but we would never have made it this far without you. Thank you from the bottom of our hearts.

HELEN

If the subject matter of any chapter in this book would make Helen cringe, it would be this one. But I think it's important to understand the kind of person she was.

When I first met Helen, she was very shy and had little self confidence, nowadays it might be said that she had low self esteem. She never expected our romance to last more than a few weeks. She was convinced that I'd find her too quiet and boring, and would 'soon be going back to my old girlfriend'.

It's true, she *was* quiet, but not with me and certainly not in a boring way - and I was never going back. More importantly, I couldn't have had a serious relationship with anyone who didn't make me laugh. Helen was hilarious. Not in a brash, attention grabbing way, she was just naturally funny. I'm sure that friends would testify that when conversation could sometimes be loud and raucous, Helen would sit quietly, smiling, taking it all in - and then come out with an amazing 'one liner', which would have everyone in fits. She had the cheekiest and sexiest giggle imaginable, *(something I miss so much).* Her smile could melt ice.

When I first saw her, I thought she was the most gorgeous thing I'd ever seen. Natural beauty, amazing hair, a great figure - and the most incredible eyes. We often joked that the first thing I fell in love with was her eyes, Helen's response always being, 'So what was wrong with the rest of me?' The fact was, absolutely nothing. She turned heads.

She also had great style. I used to tell her that she looked really good in cheap clothes – and although she would poke her tongue out at me, I think she knew what I meant!

Bizarrely Helen didn't believe herself to be the slightest bit attractive. She thought her looks were very average, she wasn't fishing for compliments, she genuinely felt that way. My chronicle of photographs is not only proof of Helen the young girl being beautiful, but Helen the woman developing into an absolute stunner. The fact that she was never aware of her good looks only made her even more irresistible.

Luckily her beauty wasn't skin deep. Helen was the kindest person I have ever met in my life. Everyone, from our two year old grandchildren to my ninety six year old mum would agree. She worried more about other people than she did herself. Helen was a naturally good person.

In her final months, her main concern was how family and friends would cope when she'd gone, myself in particular. When people visited her in her final week, she put on such a brave face that it broke my heart to watch. When my dear old mum, (who absolutely adored her), went to see her for what she knew was going to be the last time, Helen welcomed her with a big smile and...'Hello Gwennie, how are you?'.

***

Helen was 'unspoilt' and quite unique. She was very bright, but could also be amazingly naïve, (which was incredibly cute).

I think, because most of her working life she worked from home, she never had to face the sometimes unpleasant aspects of the real world. Apart from a few casual jobs, she worked alone. Illustration work was sent to her by a London agency, they handled the 'business' side of things, then she'd work off their brief. She rarely had to speak to the clients – which suited her just fine!

I'm glad she never had to face the 'bitchiness' and politics of working in an office. I think her solitary working environment contributed to her lovely innocent disposition, I'm not sure how she'd have coped in the conventional workplace. But then again, I expect she would have proved me wrong and been incredibly successful - that was Helen, full of surprises.

There was a quality about Helen which made people want to protect her. She could appear very fragile at times. She was incredibly sensitive and very easily hurt. But despite her vulnerability, she was extremely resilient. She held very strong views about life and love. She couldn't be influenced or swayed, Helen stuck to her convictions. She also had an amazing inner strength. She didn't seem afraid of death. She was angry that her body was letting her down, and bitter that she wasn't going to see the grandchildren grow up and marry, but throughout her illness, she didn't seem scared. I honestly think she thought she could beat the disease – I suppose that's what kept her going. Her Kindle is packed with books on 'how to live longer with cancer' - not books about dying.

***

Helen was an amazing illustrator. When she was four years old, she'd been bought an Enid Blyton book, loved the illustrations, and decided that was what she 'wanted to do' when she grew up. She never wavered. Academically she was frighteningly clever and was advised against taking up such a precarious profession, but Helen was strong minded, (*stubborn*) and an illustrator she became – and a very good one. I remember the joy on her face when she was commissioned to paint her first Enid Blyton story. Her childhood dream had come true.

***

We had an amazing marriage. Like many marriages, it wasn't always plain sailing, but we had a love which could endure anything that life threw at us. We were both self-employed, which meant our existence was very much 'feast or famine' - and mostly the latter!

Our love was equal. We were incredibly strong together. Helen was still quiet, even after thirty odd years of marriage, but she did become more confident. I believe that because she knew she was loved by so many, she acquired a strength and self belief which wasn't there when she was younger.

***

By the time we met the vicar to organise the funeral service, I had my ideas planned out and printed in triplicate. Our daughter didn't want it to be 'all about God, but about love and her mum'. Our son wanted to design her 'Order of Service' and write and read his own personal dedication. Helen had wanted James Taylor's 'Shower the People' to be played. The service wasn't to be a celebration of her life – there was nothing to celebrate, she shouldn't have died. Her life was incomplete, just like some of the paintings I found in her studio.

The lovely lady vicar obviously saw the strength in our family bond and generously suggested that she would just 'man the proceedings'. In that single statement she did more for my view of 'The Church' than she will ever know. She gave the 'body' she was representing a very human and defined reason for existing. She earned the respect of a non believer, a Christian and someone who hadn't got a bloody clue!

Over two hundred people attended the service to say their last goodbyes. I specifically asked for the funeral director who had organised my Dad's funeral to oversee the proceedings. He had a wonderful ability to be respectful and sombre when needed, but also knew when a bit of levity might help the proceedings along.

*When the cortege arrived at the church, he came over, shook my hand, smiled and said, 'She would be so proud....it's f***ing rammed in there!' I wasn't surprised – but it was heartening to hear it.*

We walked into the church, her family, to the strains of George Harrison singing 'Something' – a song chosen because it summed her up so well. I didn't, I couldn't look, but I'm told that virtually everybody, including most of the men, were in tears.

***

Helen wasn't perfect, however I might be painting the picture, but she was pretty damned close. She could be very single minded. She was untidy. She worried about things that she had no control over. Sometimes she'd start a painting which was absolutely brilliant – and then start again, because she didn't like it. She was her biggest critic. But those aren't faults – they are just a part of the woman I adored – and I wouldn't have changed a thing about her.

If you ever had the good fortune to meet her - and she'd let you get close enough to know her, the chances are pretty high that you'd love her. Men wanted to look after her. Women wanted to be more like her. A very good female friend summed up Helen's effect on people brilliantly :

'Most husbands were a little bit in love with Helen, but we didn't mind, because we knew she wasn't a threat'

FACEBOOK POST September 8th 2020
Helen's Birthday

Andy Smith
8 September ·

Happy Birthday Darling.
Today you would have reached the ripe old of of 58.
But you will always be 56.
Always the beautiful woman who loved to laugh, loved life and was loved by so many.
I still feel bitter that you were stolen from us, but I also feel incredibly grateful to have spent the best 35 years of my life....with you.
I've been remembering birthdays from the past.
In our courting days I would have caught the train to Manchester and we would go to our favourite Italian Restaurant in Oldham – Marios....that was the place you made me 'get down on bended knee' to ask you to marry me...even though you'd said 'Yes' months before!
You'd have a Margherita and I'd have Lasagne!
When the kids were small – we'd most likely stay at home – have cake with them and then get a takeaway.
In more recent years – you used to love to go to Jasmine Court for a wonderful Chinese feast. We always ordered too many starters – and struggled to face the main course!
I expect we would have gone there tonight if you'd been here.
You'd have spent the day with the family – and definitely seen the little ones...who no doubt would have made cards for Nanna......and we'd have spoilt you silly!

ECHOES

I'm sure that anyone who has lost someone they love will understand when I talk about 'echoes'. These aren't messages, they are more like footprints. Often, they are palpable. They have mass. Normal, everyday things that bond an incredible connection with your loss, sometimes to such an extent, that they almost become living. Unfortunately, echoes are finite and eventually there will be no more to find.

Luckily, like I mentioned earlier, Helen fell just short of being perfect by her untidiness. Her studio took over a week to sort through, but among all the piles and boxes of paper, I found some amazing artwork which I had never seen before.

When I cleared her garden workroom, I found unfinished portraits of our children and paintings of the town where her parents lived.

In her university portfolio I found a letter I'd sent her very early on in our relationship, as well as an unfinished painting of a 'very young' me! There were literally thousands of photos of friends and family, posing for what would eventually be book jackets or magazine stories, including some of her. I found three hundred pounds stuffed behind a book case. *(We never had any spare cash, God only knows where that came from.)* I discovered a voucher sent by her agent when she was told that her cancer had returned – which she hadn't spent. There were birthday cards, Valentine cards, shopping Lists. The echoes just kept coming.

***

When I sifted through the artwork of her portfolio, I found a card. It had been sent on the last day of her Art Foundation year in Manchester – she would have been nineteen. It was from someone called Colin.

It was very innocent, lots of funny little asides and cartoons - and obviously a lot of affection. I remember thinking how sweet it was and that he was probably a secret, or not so secret admirer!

It was weird, I kept going back to this teenager's card which had been sent almost half a decade ago. It haunted me, (it's still on display in our lounge). I hate loose ends.

On the reverse of the card, Colin had written his new university address and home phone number - just in case!

After much deliberation and a couple of glasses of wine, I decided to call the number. I expected it to be either 'no longer available', or a complete stranger. It was forty years ago.

I dialed. It was answered almost immediately by what sounded like a rather elderly lady. I apologised and stuttered a virtually incoherent explanation about how my wife had died and I'd found a card from someone called Colin - and I don't suppose she knew if anyone had ever lived at their address called that?

'Oh yes my dear, Colin's my son. I remember him talking about Helen. I'm so sorry. ' - I couldn't believe it!

She was very keen to give me Colin's number. I explained that I didn't want to intrude on his life, but if she could tell him, I'd be very grateful. I suggested that if I gave her my telephone number and he wanted to call me, that would be lovely, but really not necessary. The loose end had been tied.

The following morning Colin called. He told me that he'd been an unhappy teenager with very few friends, but when he met Helen and her gang on the Foundation Course, he finally felt accepted for the person he was - Colin was gay.

He was genuinely upset, but spoke with such affection for someone who had been kind to him at a time of his life when kindness was desperately needed. He was happy that she'd had a good life and was grateful that she'd been a part of his when he'd felt so alone. It epitomised Helen – and made me very proud.

***

I found a card that my mum sent to Helen on our wedding day, welcoming her into the family, and I found the letter I sent her the morning of our wedding, telling her how much I loved her and that I was the luckiest man in the world. I truly was.

***

I remember my first night, sleeping in our bed after Helen had died. Understandably, it was a very disturbed and sleepless few hours. The following morning, I asked my daughter and daughter-in-law to 'box up' the memories on Helen's dressing table – it was just too much. But that evening, I emptied the box and put everything back. It was harder to cope without, than with - and a great lesson to give myself time.

I was told not to make any big decisions for at least twelve months. It was excellent advice, but I would actually go further and say that fifteen months down the line, I still wouldn't trust my judgement - and so our bedroom remains the same, her jewellery and make-up on the dressing table, her dressing gown hanging on the wardrobe door, her nightdress on the stool, her slippers still by the bed. These are my personal 'echoes'. I'm sure some people will find it odd, but with all due respect, they aren't me, and they aren't where I am...

***

A song on the radio, her favourite TV programme, a new Lee Child's book. They all remind me of Helen. So often it's the simple, mundane things that spark a beautiful memory. I could write a book!

***

The beauty of most echoes is that you can keep going back to them. They become both comfort and friend. I frequently read text messages that Helen sent me. They are both sad and reassuring. Like a photograph, they take you back to a time or a place. Invariably they end with 'I love you' and that is always good to read.

We had a WhatsApp 'Helen updates' group where I was able to contact our children – keeping them posted on her daily health - and attitude! *(We were able to discuss things we wouldn't have wanted Helen to worry about).* She knew we had the group, she wasn't happy about it, but she sort of understood. Again, it's like a diary. I can remember how we were feeling - and our increasing concern as her condition deteriorated on a daily basis.

Occasionally I will charge Helen's phone and read messages that she sent and received. I sometimes feel guilty, it's like rifling through her handbag, but it's also a means of feeling closer to her - and so I don't think she'd mind.

***

During our thirty month engagement, we wrote to each other on a regular basis. I still have the letters Helen sent me. There are over a hundred. I will write about them more in a later chapter, but reading them is much more than an echo, it's like having her sat beside me talking about her week, telling me how much she loves me and how she misses me.

She drew funny little pictures and wrote silly poems. She worried that *'something'* would happen to one of us and she told me not to go on the back of my mates motorbike. She promised to love me 'forever and ever'.

Sadly, Helen threw away the letters that I wrote to her. It must be over twenty years ago, but I remember her saying that she didn't want anyone reading them after she was 'dead and gone', a couple have survived, but purely by chance and not design.

After Helen's death, I couldn't honestly remember what had happened to the letters she'd sent me. I expected that she'd disposed of those too. It was a great relief to find them stored in a box in the attic.

The letters are a beautiful 'echo'. As I've read them, I've marked each envelope with either a 'tick' or a 'cross'. After I've died, I don't mind if our children read the ticked ones, they tell a beautiful story, but the contents of the 'crossed' envelopes are for my eyes only, they are very personal and were only ever meant to be read by me. I know that my wishes will be respected. They are one of my favourite reminders of her.

***

Sadly, the 'echo' I most longed to find was a recent letter.

A letter telling me that she loved me and that she'd enjoyed her life. Words saying that she wouldn't have changed a thing. A reassurance that I'd done okay as a husband. But she never had the chance.

Would she have written a letter? I'll never know, but I think she might have. I'd definitely have written one to her. There were so many things that it was impossible to say towards the end, writing them in a letter might have been easier - for both of us. Sometimes, words aren't needed. But it would have been the best of 'echoes'.

FACEBOOK POST 8th January 2020

late night ramblings

Andy Smith
8 January ·

In the last 24 hours I've said...'Guess what?'....'Who was the kind friend?'....What should i do with all your clothes?....'Where did you put..?'....
Questions which will never be answered.
But ultimately, I miss you like f*** and it doesn't really matter...
I'm slowly making a start on sorting out the 'echoes' of your life...and it's really hard.....
I see a shopping list...which makes me more sad than a picture you spent hours painting - So why's that?
I suppose it's the normality of life - which is what we loved ....me and you....and the kids...your precious family.
We were there till the end...and i know that would have been important to you.....It was for us too.
I will probably remove this post in the morning- i might not..but maybe.... Not because i'm ashamed of what i feel...but because i've said what i want to say.

A special find

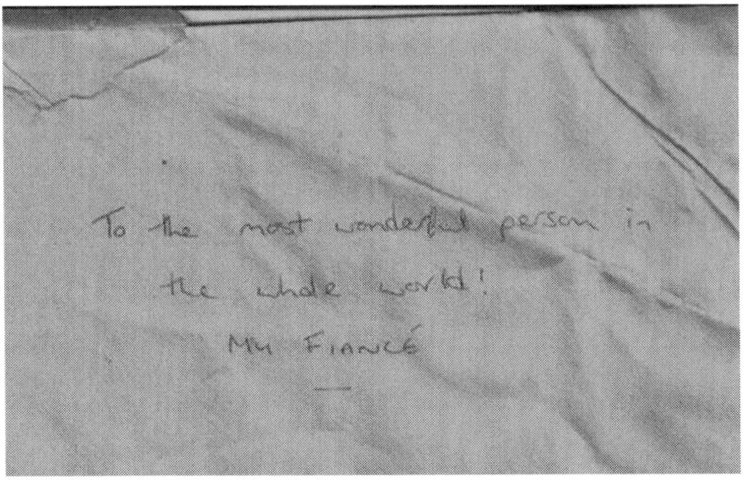

ANGER

There are several stages of grief – just how many is a mute point, but one of those stages is 'Anger'. This is a stage I'm very aware of. My anger started a long time before Helen died. I'll never forget the evening she told me 'we weren't going to grow old and grey together'.

Helen had her three monthly appointment with the results of her regular scan – I had a gig in Shropshire - and so I was unable to go with her. Luckily, our daughter-in-law said that she'd take her – thank God she did.

In the three months since her previous scan, the cancer had returned in a big way. They were going to give her twelve weeks of chemotherapy, but it could only be palliative treatment – and hopefully it would hold the spread at bay, and give her, (and us) a bit more time..

I was totally unaware of the news. I was desperately trying to contact her to tell her I'd arrived at my gig and check that the results were still clear. Eventually, five minutes before going on stage, I tracked her down. She told me things weren't good, (I knew by her voice). She'd tell me when I got home.

I did my gig on 'auto pilot' and drove back to Rugby like an idiot, breaking every speed limit imaginable. I arrived home about eleven o'clock – she was sat on the settee. She held my hand and told me.

The following day I went to work – I opened my shop. Both our son and daughter called in and we cried together. I couldn't accept what I'd been told, I went into denial – another accepted stage of grief – a stage I'm still in. In fairness, my mind wasn't on my work and I popped upstairs to my studio, leaving the shop unattended. When I came down a few minutes later, I realised that my mobile phone had been stolen. I know who stole it, my neighbouring shop knew – but the police didn't follow it up and I not only lost my phone, but more importantly, I lost my messages and countless photos of Helen – my echoes banked for the future.

In normal circumstances, I'd accept that I'd been careless. Not a chance! My phone had been stolen by a local drug addict, who sold it immediately for fifty pounds. For a while, my anger was concentrated on him. How dare he exist, him and his worthless life? My beautiful, blameless wife was going to die, why not him? I wanted to kill him. In fairness, (I don't need to, he's making a pretty good job of doing that to himself anyway), but this was the first sign of 'anger' creeping in – I needed to blame someone. He was an easy target.

***

After Helen's death, my life was a kaleidoscope of emotions. Initially I didn't feel anger, I felt totally numb, and an enormous sense of loss and sadness. The truth didn't seem possible. It took seven days for the anger to really kick in.

As children, both Helen and me were brought up in religious families. However much you think you change as you grow up, these things stay with you. I believe in God, but I don't believe that going to church on a Sunday is a passport to Heaven. I personally believe that leading a good life should guarantee a beautiful afterlife.

Through the whole of Helen's illness and treatment I'd prayed to God. I'd bargained with God. But seven days after she died – my anger turned on him. Why hadn't he answered my prayers? How could he do this to our family? Couldn't he have picked someone else? She was fifty six years old for Christ's sake!

Why did he make her suffer? Why did he make her children watch her die? Why didn't he at least try to justify what he'd done to us? Did he hate us so much? Were we worth so little to him? I got no reply.

I wrote a very angry post on Facebook. I remember waking in the middle of the night and thinking…'Oh no, I'd better 'take it down'. But already people had started posting comments of support, I decided to let it stay. I'm pleased I did. It's very powerful, very emotional and very sad. It still moves me and I can vividly remember pouring out my pain on that Saturday evening. That night it hit me like a truck – and the grieving really started.

Over the last twelve months, I've had numerous one sided conversations with God. I'm less bitter, but I'm still angry. I can't forgive him - and on my day of reckoning, I'll be wanting some answers. Would it be easier if I didn't believe? Who knows?

***

I met some very good friends for a meal a couple of months after Helen died. We decided to meet at a nearby pub before moving on to the restaurant.

They'd been there to support her during her illness, they'd sent me a card and they came to the funeral. They did all those things that people are 'expected' to do, but we sat for an hour and Helen's name wasn't mentioned. The conversation was flowing, but I became increasingly annoyed with them. I hope I was hiding my anger and frustration, but by the time we moved on to the restaurant, I was ready to head home and cross them off my Christmas card list.

We were shown to our table and ordered our food - and then she asked, 'Do you mind if we talk about Helen? We don't want to upset you, but we'd like to if you feel up to it'.

They were trying to protect me. They wanted to talk about the events leading up to Helen's death – and they were concerned for me and how I was coping without her.

They just weren't sure if I'd want to talk about it. I had resented what I read to be their total lack of interest, compassion and love. I was angry, needlessly. Nowadays, Helen is a part of my conversation from the outset. Hopefully it makes life easier for everybody.

Being on different wavelengths when grieving is very common. Rational thinking is no longer part of the equation. I was taught a very important lesson. It's uncharted waters. It's eggshells. It's a very unsteady balancing act. Few people know what to do or say – it's awkward and in a similar situation – I might well do the same thing, even now.

***

My anger was/is sometimes totally irrational. I became annoyed seeing couples together. Particularly old couples. Watching them walking hand in hand started bugging me. I know where it came from, that was obvious, but it wasn't fair.

I started to resent the marriages of our friends. Suddenly it was odd numbers - couples and me. They were happy – I wasn't. It made life difficult for a while. Everybody seemed to have someone to love – apart from me. I still struggle when there's an unoccupied chair in a restaurant, or at a friend's house. Helen's chair. The stupid thing is that I'm not alone, everybody sat around the table is missing her. It might not be mentioned, but the unspoken sadness is there, and always will be. It's very easy to be selfish – but it is also forgivable.

I don't begrudge anybody a long and happy married life, I just wish that twenty years down the line, *we* could have been the old and grey-haired couple, holding hands, aimlessly strolling around town.

I'm just jealous!

FACEBOOK POST 10th August 2019
seven days after Helen died

> **Andy Smith**
> 10 August 2019 ·
>
> Watching the last couple of recordings of 'Killing Eve' on my own.
> It wasn't meant to be this way.
> Giving God a much deserved hard time tonight. Can't help but feel he's got a touch complacent and unforgivingly, guilty of sleeping on the job. Crap performance Mr Almighty!
> Thankful for friends and family who have shown far more love and kindness than any 'so-called' compassionate omnipresent disappointment.

WANTING TO BELIEVE IN GHOSTS

I was quite surprised when I read Sasha Bates's book that she often felt the presence of her late husband. She's a psychotherapist, it wasn't what I expected to read.

She argued that if people are sceptical and think it's 'all in your mind', it doesn't matter. If it help you handle your loss, it can't be a bad thing. I agree. As a bereaved husband, I will cling on to any possibility that Helen is still 'out there somewhere' and contacting me, however ridiculous it might sound.

(If you want to skip to the next chapter, I totally understand. But I felt I had to include my dialogue with Helen since she'd died. It's been an integral part of handling her death and facing my new life.)

When my dad died a few years ago – I wanted him to send me a message. The problem was that I was trying to orchestrate the conversation. We had a lamp in our lounge and I wanted him to make it flash. I would sit in the dark, night after night - waiting. Of course it didn't. I made a big mistake. *Sorry Dad, not your fault.*

***

I'm no expert, but I've learnt that you have to be 'in tune' to the signals. God knows how it works. I can only compare it to a dodgy internet connection. I'm sure there have been occasions when I've missed her messages – I hope not too often.

I had my first sign eight days after Helen passed away. I was alone for the first time in a week. I decided I needed music to break the deadly silence. Helen had bought me a record deck a couple of Christmases ago and I thought it would be nice to play some vinyl. I didn't care what I played, I just needed noise!

I delved into my collection and pulled out an album I hadn't listened to in decades, The Furey's, 'When You Were Sweet Sixteen'. I didn't even check which side I was playing, (actually it was side two), I just whacked it on the turntable and turned up the volume. The lyric of the first song I'd listened to for several weeks went : *'I will love you, I will love you, when I am gone'.* I fell apart.

***

Times have changed, even since losing my dad. Now when someone dies, the funeral home automatically set up a web page notifying loved ones of funeral details..etc..etc. There is also a facility to donate to a favoured charity and an opportunity to build an online photograph album.

I spent hours looking through our old photos, which was both sad and lovely. I created a file on my computer and started scanning, uploading and posting some beautiful pictures of Helen. All was going swimmingly well until....

I had a few photos from our honeymoon in the very hot summer of 1986. Helen is posing on the beach in a tiny little bikini, suntanned, twenty five years old and gorgeous! I was very aware, whilst scanning, that Helen wouldn't approve of my posting them on the website, but she looked lovely and I wanted to share them. The moment I tried to upload to the site, my computer screen rolled and went black. It stayed that way for over twenty four hours - and then it returned to normal. No explanation. No reason. Just Helen making her feelings known!

***

I frequently dream about Helen. Usually I wake up, aware that she was a part of it and I struggle to remember the context.

One night, I woke knowing that she'd been in my dream, I tried to remember the scenario, but it was muddled. I rolled over and she was there, laid beside me. I touched her, I felt her skin. I felt her warmth. I smelt Helen...

Dreams fade - usually before I wake, but this is still as real as any memory I have of a 'living' Helen. I think she was there. Actually, I 'm sure she was. I long for it to happen again – but I don't think it will.

***

As I mentioned earlier, we had a long distance relationship when we first met. Helen was a student in Manchester, I was a penniless musician in Rugby. But we wrote to each other. I have over a hundred love letters and they are probably my most valued possession. They will be buried with me. I read them to her when I visit the cemetery - and I'm on my fourth time round.

Each letter is numbered and stored in date order in a long box. As each letter is taken out, the next one is turned ready for the following day. I'm so OCD about it!

A few months ago, I'd had a very bad day. I wept by her graveside and begged her to send a sign that she was okay. I needed to know that she was still a part of our torn lives and was watching over us. I read her letter and went home. When I came to put it back in the box, I realised that I'd read the wrong one, the letter I should have read was missing. I became manic, I checked bins, I pulled the house to pieces. I went to bed more than a little distressed.

The following morning, I returned to the box of letters, *(which I'd already been through several times),* I'd lost letter number five. I eventually found it mixed in with the seventies - that couldn't happen! I was so relieved that I took it into our bedroom and read it straight away.

It's hard to explain. But Helen's letters were very funny, and 'very Helen'. On the first page of this letter she'd stuck a photo of her stunningly beautiful eyes....and next to them she'd written...'I'm keeping an eye on you'.

sorry about the greasy finger marks: I've just had a piece of toast!
I'm keeping an eye on you.
Hello Darling

***

When we first met, if we were in company, we used to squeeze each others hand three times *I..LOVE..YOU.* It was our little secret signal. We used it for over thirty years. I now feel like we have another.

It first happened a few months ago. I was in the shower, the water was warm, but I suddenly felt icy cold and shivered uncontrollably in the heat. It now happens on a regular basis.

Yesterday I was driving to Hunstanton for a few days break – the sun was shining – it was a beautiful day. I was talking to Helen and telling her I'd be okay this time. (It was my second visit since her death.) I started shivering, to the point where I should probably have stopped driving. Her presence was so immense. She couldn't have been more beside me if she'd been sat in the passenger seat.

***

Embarrassingly, we had pet names for each other. Helen was a ferret (for reasons not required) and I was a mole - because I look like one (allegedly)!

I'm a great believer that young children are far more open to messages from beyond than adults. I have a very special bond with both our grandchildren and they talk about Helen as if she's still here. Who knows what they see. I'd had a very difficult few days and again, I'd asked Helen for a sign...

I usually put my grandson to bed on a Tuesday night. This involves getting very wet at bath-time and then reading the bedtime story. The story of the night's main protagonist was a dog. I'd read it numerous times before, it's one of his favourite books. But when I started reading to him he stopped me short.

'Grandad. Not a dog - can it be a mole tonight?' and so the dog became a mole for the whole story. It had never happened before and it hasn't happened since. He went to sleep a happy little two year old and I felt like my request had been played.

***

Like I say, it could all be wishful thinking on my part. Just me hanging on to anything that might, however unlikely, indicate that she's still nearby.

Coincidences? Maybe. But I'd prefer to think that Helen really is sending her cryptic messages. Perhaps she actually is watching over her family and the people she loved - and is also quietly giggling in the knowledge that you now know she thought I looked like a mole!

FACEBOOK POST 11th November 2019

Andy Smith is with **Helen Smith**.
11 November 2019 ·

Sometimes the evenings are very dark and lonely - and then i feel her stood by my side, with a hand on my shoulder, telling me it's going to be alright and i'm doing ok....even if i'm not.

MAKING MEMORIES

Shortly after Helen's diagnosis, we were taken into a windowless room and told about the support she would receive from both the hospital and Macmillan's Nurses. I remember being told that we needed to go away and make memories.

To be honest, I felt a bit annoyed. We'd been making memories for over thirty years, what right had they to say that now was the time to start? Helen said nothing. But actually, as so often happens, I was proved wrong.

Helen soon came up with a list of things she wanted to do. I still have it. She enjoyed searching the internet for places to stay. She went shopping for new clothes. She contacted friends and family, hoping that they were able to accommodate the dates she'd scribbled down. Amazingly, she made planning the last few months of her life seem like the most natural thing in the world. She was remarkably brave.

We booked a week at our friend's caravan in Hunstanton, where she was dumbstruck to find our holiday friends rolling up for a couple of nights unannounced. *(It was something that she'd tried to plan herself, but they'd joined in my subterfuge and told her that they couldn't make it)*. She collapsed on the floor with joy when they arrived. It was a memory I'll take with me to my grave. It poured with rain for most of our visit – but it didn't matter, we were together.

***

We caught a train to Liverpool for the Easter Bank Holiday with a group of special friends – the weather was sublime. We enjoyed all 'The Beatles' things that we'd done years before, but with a knowledge that we wouldn't be doing them again. Either of us.

We ate, we drank, we went to the theatre, we laughed. She sang and danced her little heart out at The Cavern Club - and for a few days - because she was so alive - it was easy to forget that the clock was ticking. We all forgot.

***

We hadn't been home forty eight hours before we headed off to the Cotswolds for a few days with her cousin, best school friend and respective husbands.

Again, it was perfection, and a pleasure to see the joy on Helen's face as we laughed at old photographs, ate, walked and talked about old times. I'm sure there were occasions when we all had a *'this won't happen again'* feeling, but Helen was in such a lovely, chilled mood, it was impossible to dwell on what was around the corner.

***

At the beginning of June we went to our friend's son's wedding in Chester. It was an Indian Wedding and she was very excited about the prospect of going. She bought a new dress, handbag and shoes. We were very aware that it was in the lap of the gods whether we'd make it or not, but we went. It was a long, but beautiful day and Helen lasted from start to end. She was visibly tired when we got back to our accommodation, but she was so pleased that she'd felt well enough to go, and it was another box ticked.

***

Her biggest 'Making Memories' wish was her last holiday. Unsurprisingly, she wanted to spend some time with the family. We booked a lovely house in Seaton, Devon.

Our car broke down an hour before we were due to leave home. I remember rolling up at the front door and collapsing in tears and desperation. She hugged me. She was the strong one, I was weak. I was obviously struggling far more than I realised. Luckily, after a few phone calls, our children pulled together and we were transported to Devon.

It was during that holiday that we started noticing how poorly she was. She struggled to walk any distance, she disappeared to bed during the day. She was quieter.

Her best friend and husband, who now live in Dorset, came over for a day. We had a cream tea, and then they went shopping, just the two of them. When they arrived back at the house, we sat outside in the sunshine and chatted. They left late afternoon.

At the time I was unaware, but her friend had noticed an enormous change in Helen's appearance and health. It was something that was more gradual for us, but a shock for her. I think I'm right in saying that they were forced to stop on their journey home because she feared she would never see her best friend again.

She did, once more, just in time. Thank God.

Returning to the 'Making Memories' advice. It was so right! Not because the memories made before hadn't counted, they had made our marriage what it was, but when you know that everything you do together might be the last time, the whole perspective changes.

I know that Helen treasured those last few months. She was surrounded by special people who were the centre of her life. She wasn't sad, at least she didn't seem to be. She defied death with her love for living.

I often look back at photographs from those last few months, and she radiates something beyond beauty and strength, she radiates love. A love for me, the children, her grandchildren, her family, her friends - and a love for her all too short life.

Truthfully, the photos *are* a testament of her gradual decline – but I can honestly say that those close to her, who saw her on a daily basis, didn't notice, probably because we didn't want to.

I hate to admit it – but the Macmillan's nurse was bang on! Whenever I need something to get me through the day, the chances are pretty high that it will be 'a clip' from those last few months. Something from our 'Making Memories' scrap book.

***

When it was suggested back in March 2019, I thought it was a suggestion for Helen's benefit, which it was, but it was so much more for the ones who were going to be left behind. We were the ones who would appreciate those special days and hours for the rest of our lives. At that point, regardless of money, work, the future, the past, we had one communal mindset - the only thing that mattered was Helen.

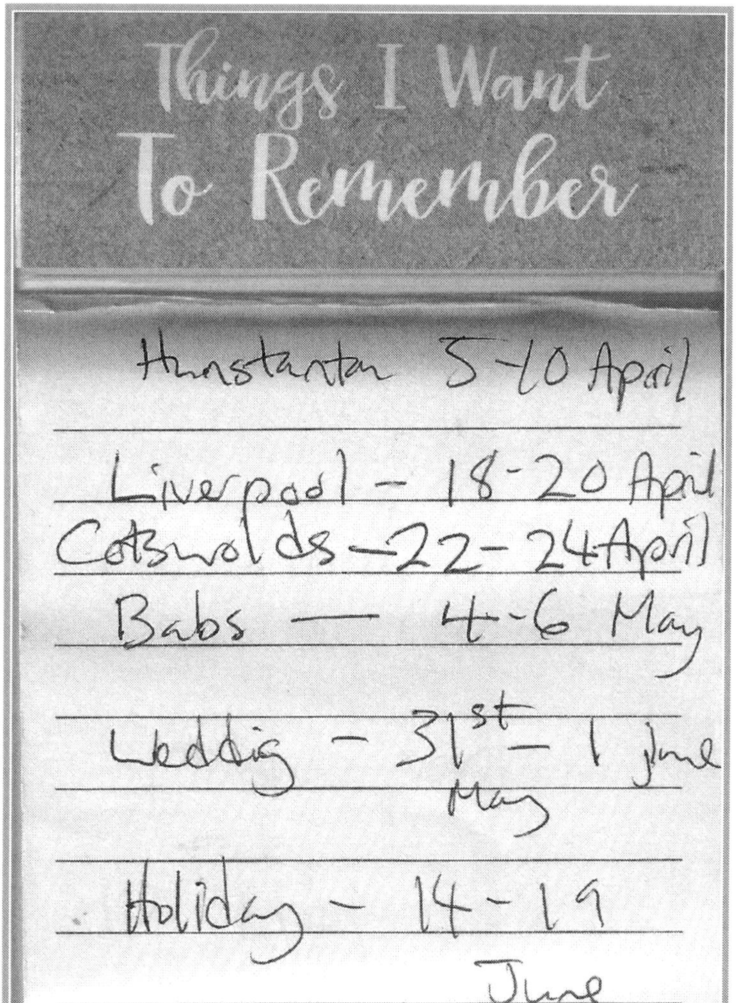

Things I Want To Remember
Hunstanton 5-10 April
Liverpool - 18-20 April
Cotswolds - 22-24 April
Babs — 4-6 May
Wedding - 31st May - 1 June
Holiday - 14-19 June

THE FINAL DAYS

The last few days of Helen's life are a blur, but also a memory ingrained for eternity.

When we were told that she wasn't expected to last until the end of the week, I understandably fell apart. It's difficult to know how Helen felt, after the initial tears, she retreated into herself. I suppose she was preparing for whatever lay ahead. I've learnt since that it's called 'detachment', the dying person needs to put a space between themselves and the people they love. Ironically, it's a survival instinct – as much for the dying, as for those remaining.

We planned to spend the May Day Bank Holiday in Sutton Coldfield with our holiday friends. (These were people we'd met fifteen years earlier on a Devon holiday, and who we continued to holiday with and meet several times a year.) We had a really enjoyable day at The Black Country Museum, and the following day went for a lovely walk in Sutton Park, followed by a few beers in the nearby pub. I have to say, I'm not a big drinker, and struggle to keep up with our friends, but Helen seemed so well, the sun was shining, so what the hell!

In the evening we were meeting for a curry, but before eating, we had a couple of drinks in a pub close to our hotel. The meal was delicious, washed down with a few bottles of wine and lots of laughter. Afterwards, we went to a hostelry over the road...

By this point I was struggling to focus on the easiest route to the Gents - and I'd gone very quiet. I was 'helped' back to the hotel where I prepared for my evening ablutions. It seems Helen heard an almighty crash, and found me falling backwards into the bath with my legs hanging over the side. Not my coolest of moves. She pulled me out and helped me get ready for bed. I remember taking her in my arms – and as drunk as I was – or because I was – I burst into tears and told her that I didn't want her to die. She held me very tight. She never mentioned the episode again. Ten weeks later she was gone.

I remember when my dad was dying. We held his hand, stroked his hair, we told him how much we loved him. But we were waiting for the inevitable. He needed no painkillers, he didn't suffer – he slipped away. He was ninety one.

Helen was a very different ball game. I stayed with her day and night for over one hundred hours, witnessing, with our children, the worst nightmare imaginable. The staff at the hospice were incredible, but they couldn't save her. It's a terrible thing to say or feel, but by the third day, we were almost willing her to let go.

To watch the person you love more than anything in the world suffer is beyond any Hell. Hopefully the drugs were doing their job - I pray that the pain in her eyes wasn't manifested in her body. Helen hung on to life in a way that we knew she would. My beautiful, strong, but stubborn wife.

In her final moments I sat with her, with our children, holding her hand, telling her we loved her, trying to hold it together, but not managing particularly well. Within seconds of her dying, her body changed. The pain in her face disappeared and she looked at peace. She could have been twenty one again – it was an incredible transformation.

When I went to see her in the funeral home, she looked 'like Helen'. I went to see her often, far too often. Family members and friends became concerned. I needed to let go. I knew I did, I could see where this was going to end – and it wasn't a good place. Reluctantly, seven days before the funeral, I went to see her for the last time.

Arguably it was just a body, it wasn't Helen. But in my mind it *was* Helen. It was the body I'd danced with in 1983. It was the body I'd made love to, and the body that gave birth to our children. It was the body that took hours to get ready to go out for an evening. It was the body of the person I had worshipped for over thirty years, and no, it wasn't 'Helen the person' – but it was as close as I was able to get.

Helen came home for her last night the afternoon before

the day of her funeral. Because I'd spent so much time with her dead body, it seemed like a natural thing to do. It wasn't weird, it was a comfort to have her nearby. I talked to her, I sang to her. I read one of her letters and I drank a glass of red wine with her. We slept together, in the same room, under our roof for the last time.

Understandably, there was considerable concern for my mental health and my ability to cope with such an unorthodox situation, but we spent a very beautiful evening together. Those were hours which I will never forget, or regret. I honestly feel they gave me the strength to face the funeral. How could that be wrong?

Andy Smith
29 August ·

At 4.00pm on August 29th 2019 Helen came home.
I'd promised her that she would – and she did.
We spent the evening together.
I had a glass of wine. I sang her a song. I read one of her old letters and I told her how I didn't know how I could live without her.
I went to sleep beside her.
I woke in the middle of the night to see her coffin silhouetted against the night sky – it was both surreal and cruel – but not frightening...it was Helen for Christ's sake!
The following day she was buried at Whinfield cemetery – near to the park where the grandchildren play – and a place close to her heart.

We all dreaded the funeral, but despite it being unbelievably sad, it was a day of great pride.
Over 200 people came to say goodbye...
Friends, family...people who were there for me....packed St Johns Church and gave her the send off she so richly deserved.
Our children stood up at the front of the church and gave incredibly personal testaments of love for their mum...something I was totally unable to do...but they did...and I couldn't have been more proud!

12 months on...still angry, still lost, still missing my best friend.
Still hearing a song and thinking of her.
Still thinking she'll be there watching 'Bargain Hunt' when I walk through the front door.
Still amazed that she fell in love with me in the first place!
Still lonely, despite being surrounded by the best friends and family....but it's not 'loneliness'..it's 'Helen–lessness'....and no-one or anything can fill that gaping chasm.

I'm lucky in so many ways.
Little people have made me laugh, not forget, but made me realise that I still have a reason to carry on.
Helen clung on to life until her very last breath – and so I need to value the fact that I can wake in the morning and try to make a difference...
I'm not saying that there won't be days when I won't want to get out of bed, because there will.....
Some days I will be selfish, ignore phone calls and messages and just want to be on my own...with her....like it used to be....

This is the 'last, first' today – thank you for tolerating my diatribes over the last 12 months and if you are still waiting for me to reply to your voicemail – Sorry. I'm fine x

COUNSELLING

There was an occasion on the morning of her death when I struggled to hold it together. We'd had very little sleep and Helen seemed increasingly agitated and uncomfortable. She'd just had a very distressing half an hour, and whilst the nurses were trying to settle her and ease her suffering, I just dissolved. I utterly and totally lost it.

A very kind nurse called Jenny took my hand and led me out of Helen's room and sat beside me in a visitors lounge. I didn't want to leave Helen – I had visions of her dying whilst I was gone and not being there to hold her.

I apologised. Jenny brought me a cup of coffee and explained that she'd have been very surprised if I hadn't fallen apart. I was going through a darkness beyond black. This was the worst day of my life. I was trying to be strong for Helen, our children, it was little wonder that it all became too much and pushed me over the edge.

I was a snivelling, snotty mess and she showed me a kindness that you can't be taught. She was just one of those very special people. I remember telling her what a happy, close, loving family we had always been and that our children shouldn't be witnessing the death of their mum, a mum they would be lost without. I told her that it would haunt them for the rest of their lives - and mine - and sadly, I wasn't wrong.

Jenny put her arm around me and told me that when I felt ready, I might want to consider some counselling sessions. The hospice offered the facility to all family members – and even friends of loved ones who had died on their premises.

To be honest, it wasn't something that I'd have normally considered, but I knew she was right and that it might help me. I had no idea what the next few weeks and months were going to throw at us, but I was pretty sure it wasn't going to be easy or pretty. I told her I would.

She led me back to Helen's bedside.

***

It's recommended that you wait at least six weeks before starting sessions. Everything is very raw for those first few weeks after the death, apart from that, there are all the practical things to deal with, including the funeral.

After seven weeks, I made the phone call. Within a few days I was contacted and told I'd been allocated a counsellor and could start the following week. I had a choice, but I decided to return to the hospice for my sessions. It just seemed right.

I knew that walking through the door for the first time would be difficult. The last time I'd been under their roof, Helen had died an hour earlier, but I felt it was a challenge I needed to face.

On the morning of my first session, I wasn't sure that it was such a great idea after all. Was it too soon? Was I being a bit too unkind to myself?

I cried all the way along the M6, but as soon as I crossed the threshold, I knew it was the right decision. The people in this building had only ever shown us love and kindness. I knew that by coming back, I was completing the circle. There was nothing to be afraid of.

I bought a cup of coffee, (a very nice cup of coffee), from the volunteers in the cafe and waited for my counsellor. It felt a bit strange!

I don't know why, but she was younger than I expected. She smiled and led me (and my cup of coffee), up the stairs to a room with a couple of settees, tasteful décor, and a table with a box of tissues on it. *'I might need those',* I thought.

She introduced herself. Let's call her 'Pam'. She sat cross legged with a notebook and pen at the ready. She explained the format of the sessions and asked me to fill in a questionnaire about where I felt I was in the grief process. It was important that I answered honestly.

The list of questions is hazy, but they went along the lines of : 'Was I angry? Was I in denial? Was I coping? Had I had suicidal thoughts?' I answered 'yes' to most of them.

And then we started talking. Well I did! I told her about Helen, our family, our careers, how we met, our dreams. I asked her if she knew Helen's medical background, she told me she didn't. That's how it worked. They were dealing with me, not Helen. I told her anyway. She asked me some probing questions, I answered as honestly as I could. We hit it off.

Arguably, because I'm very 'heart on sleeve', I'm probably a counsellor's dream. I can talk for Britain and I'm not scared to let my heart bleed, but at the end of the day, you have to gel as human beings, and we did on that first wintry, morning meeting.

After fifty five minutes she would always say, 'We have five minutes left, are you okay?' At the end of our first session, she told me that she had been so mesmerised by our story, that she hadn't written a single word in her notebook, *(something that she always did to remind herself when writing her reports later).* She said that she'd remember everything. Straight away I knew that this was a relationship that was going to work.

We had twelve sessions in all – I would readily have had more, but I was very aware that there were other needy people waiting in the queue. I cried a lot, (*I needed those tissues*). We laughed loads. She knew every detail about my family - and I learned some things about hers.

She encouraged me to exorcise my feelings in writing. If I was struggling, I should express the chaos in my heart in a written paragraph. Keep a journal. Write a song. This book would never have been written if it hadn't have been for Pam.

On our eleventh meeting she embarrassedly asked if she could see a photo of Helen, *(something she told me she* *wouldn't normally do). S*he felt like she knew her, and wanted to put a face to the story. I showed her. She thought she was beautiful. Everybody did!

Our last meeting was always going to be quite sad. It was a bit like the last day of school. I took books that Helen had illustrated, I showed her photos of our grandchildren and children. We talked about how I hoped my future would pan out. She was always totally professional, but more importantly, she was incredibly human and kind.

***

Counselling doesn't solve the problem. Nothing can. It's not for everybody, but it certainly helped me to look at life and death from a different perspective. Her frequent response to my personal impatience would be, 'What do you think Helen would have thought? What would she have done? Would she have coped better?'

Was counselling beneficial? God yes! I told Pam things that I couldn't tell closest family or friends. Not because she didn't care, because she did, but because she wasn't a part of 'that' life, and *they* were, and cared too much.

That's why counselling works so much better than a chat with your best mate in the pub. You have to be honest, you won't be judged, but you will be supported.

On my dark days I often long to pick up the phone and talk to her again. I probably could. But I won't. That chapter needed to close.

I often wonder if I'd died first, would Helen have booked counselling sessions? It was something that Pam asked.

The truth is, I don't know. She would have benefited, without a doubt, but Helen was such a private person, I'm not sure that she would have been able to 'open up' to a stranger. In hindsight, we might have both gained something if we'd done it together, when she was ill. I'd just never considered taking that route until it was too late.

FACEBOOK POST 19th Sep 2019

The only way we can say 'Thank You'

Andy Smith is with **Helen Smith**.
19 September 2019 ·

On behalf of Helen (in her absence), myself and our family, I would like to thank all the people who have donated to Myton Hospice in her memory.
Incredibly,we have raised (with Gift Aid) £2156.02
Both the Hospice and myself, have been amazed by the generosity of all the beautiful, kind people who loved and continue to miss her.
She was a very special person in life - and even in death, has managed to do something amazing..
As a family, we will continue to raise money for 'Myton Hospice' and 'Target Ovarian Cancer' and it's good to know that we can count on your support.
Thanks again. x

COPING

Over the last fifteen months, my coping strategies have been both productive and destructive. In the few weeks after Helen's death and leading up to her funeral, I hardly stopped to take breath. When I did, my world fell apart, so I spent every waking moment ensuring that I was preoccupied.

With the help of our children, we planned the funeral service, *(which was sad but incredibly beautiful).* I scanned and printed every item of her artwork that I could lay my hands on, compiling several portfolios of her pictures for displaying at the wake. I painstakingly went through all our photograph albums, computer folders, phones and cameras, finding some of the best pictures of Helen and uploading them onto the funeral website. I tracked down old friends who I thought should be told. I pulled the house to pieces looking for a letter, a letter which I knew she hadn't written, but I looked anyway. I tried to put the last few months into some chronological order, both on paper and in my head, it was important not to forget...I just didn't stop!

Don't get me wrong, it didn't always work. Frequently I would be crying whilst printing her pictures or looking at her photos. I would sit by her side in tears at the funeral home, telling her what I'd been doing and hoping that she'd approve. I was very aware of what was happening, I just didn't know what else to do. I worried about how her death was affecting me, both then, and more frighteningly, how I was going to face the barren months ahead. I'd never lost a wife before. I didn't know how I was supposed to act. I just knew it was probably wasn't how I was acting!

I'm sure I was a pretty poor dad. My behaviour was totally self-centred. Our kids closed ranks and protected me, despite their own grief. They trusted me to look after our grandchildren, who were a beautiful distraction and the best, if only temporary remedy. Even then, Helen was never very far away - they frequently mentioned her name. I'm sure they were totally confused, and wondered where their lovely, laughing nanna had disappeared to. I was struggling to understand, so what chance did a two year old have?

I remember an afternoon, when Maisie, (our little granddaughter), spent some time with me, not long after the funeral. She noticed a photo of Helen at the other end of the lounge, she smiled with recognition and said, 'There's Nanna in her necklace', and returned to playing with the toys. I've used the lines in one of my songs – the innocence of childhood is so beautiful and so to be envied.

The months passed. We selected several of Helen's 'nursery' style paintings, which we printed, framed and sold for our charities on the lead up to Christmas. It kept me very busy and we raised over a thousand pounds..

I've decorated, *(something I'd never really done)*. I turned her garden studio into a playhouse for the grandchildren. During the summer Lockdown, I gardened and grew vegetables.

I decided to bring my recording studio home, installing it in the bedroom which had been her art studio. I started learning to speak Welsh, a crazy but beautiful language. I met friends, I did gigs, I started going to the theatre....

But however much I was trying to fill my day, there was always going to come a point when reality kicked in. I acquainted myself with a new friend. He was called 'Merlot'. I've never been a big drinker - and it's certainly not something I'd ever felt dependent on. Helen and me enjoyed sharing a bottle of wine of an evening, but when you buy a bottle just to '*feel less*' – it's a very different story.

The pain doesn't go, but it anaesthetises. It helped me sleep, and kept the nightmares away. Unfortunately, it also made me so lethargic, I didn't want to get out of bed in a morning – even after sleeping for ten hours.

Eventually, the friend became less of a friend. He outstayed his welcome. Instead of making me feel better, his company started to get on my nerves - and have the opposite effect. I'd get angry, I'd shout at the wall. Merlot was letting me down.

It's easy to see how it happened, for a while, it helped. I still indulge in a glass of red, but now I know he's not a solution and he's not worthy of my friendship. It's just a nice drink!

I recall a Monday. I'd looked after our grandson for about nine hours on my own. We'd had great fun, but it's full on, it's noisy, it's silly, it's exhausting. The house was filled with noise and laughter. We'd both had a good time.

He was collected. I waved goodbye and closed the door. I tidied away the toys and half eaten beans on toast. Suddenly our noisy house became as quiet as Helen's graveyard – I opened a bottle.

'My company tonight, appears when all the smiles have gone,

when darkness fills the sky and chills my soul'

(a lyric from 'Merlot' – Andy Smith – Before and Here After)

***

Even before Helen died, I knew that I wanted to help the hospice. They'd made the last few days of her life slightly more bearable, not only for her, but also for the family.

It was weird, but at every previous time of crisis in my life, I would turn to my guitar and my music, but it was nearly two months before I picked up a guitar with the intention of writing a new song. If I had to self-analyse, I'd say that I didn't want to write something bitter and angry, I needed to write a love song – I still loved her. It was written in Dorset, in the conservatory of her best friend's house, on their son's guitar - which seemed fitting and right - I also knew it would be the first of a few. It's called 'Long Way From Home'.

I decided that I would record and release a charity album. A selection of songs which I'd written for Helen over our thirty six year love affair, plus anything else I felt inspired to write in the aftermath. This became my new way of coping. A much better way of coping. I was doing something useful, as well as being creative and therapeutic. I'd benefit, the hospice would benefit. Helen would be smiling.

When I started the project, I'd often record into the early hours of the morning. I was doing something which was familiar to me, something I enjoyed, and something where I actually needed to be alone. It felt good re-learning the old songs and remembering when and why they were written. A few of the lyrics were very painful to read and sing, but when they were composed, we had no idea what lay ahead.

The album is almost complete, and it's something that I'm sure I'll always be proud of. It's the story of our life, and despite the sad songs, it has a really positive feel, something which I wasn't expecting. Writing this book is another way of using words to reflect how I feel, banish the demons - and raise money for our charities.

***

It's true, the black days still rear their ugly heads – and those are the days when I find it hard enough to breathe, let alone be creative. But the days when the pain can be translated into something positive are a ray of sunshine, those are my better days – that's when I'm coping.

FACEBOOK POST 18th April 2020

Andy Smith
18 April ·

Today i got up at 8.30, but i didn't shower, dress, shave, clean my teeth until 3.00 this afternoon...yes, I've turned into a tramp!!
Actually, i was working on and with some beautiful generous people who are contributing musically to my charity album.. 'Before & Here After'...
In these scary times of social distancing...the internet has found a worthy bedfellow....thank you guys for bailing me out...emailing your tracks...and making it all work.....you know who you are!
The album, with so much help from a nucleus of talent, will hopefully raise shed loads of well deserved money for 'Myton Hospice' and 'Target Ovarian Cancer'.......and be something i will be incredibly proud of for the rest of my life.
A man on a mission! x

REALITY

If I'd ever been asked what the worst thing that could happen in my life would be? The answer would have been easy. Losing Helen.

It happened, and the reality is, that a lot of the time I wish I could join her. Sometimes it would be a relief to escape the pain. It's not a physical pain, although it often feels like it is, it's a constant throbbing which comes and goes in intensity. It's always there.

There are a thousand reasons why I need to stick around and only one why I'd prefer to die, but regularly, that one reason overshadows the thousands. I would never consider suicide as a preferable option to living, but death no longer scares me. I fear dying, but that's a different issue. Actually, I don't want to die, I just want her back. The one thing I long for more than anything in this world, is unattainable. But whatever is beyond life, Helen is there – and that is the pull.

On my regular visits to the cemetery, I read the hundreds of gravestones, and particularly the ones where a husband or wife has been added at a later date. Sometimes it's just a few years, sometimes it's decades. I often wonder if the partner who was left behind felt like I do, longing to join their loved one, but knowing that it's wrong. Did they feel that pain for thirty years? Were they counting the days? I hope not. I hope I don't.

I like to believe that she's still here with me – in some spiritual form or other. But whether she is or not, the reality is that she's no longer here in the physical sense. She's dead. She's in a wooden box several feet underground. She'll be cold. She won't look like my Helen any more. Whatever our destiny together, in this lifetime I will never see her, touch her, hold her, or laugh with her again. Little wonder that I struggle.

***

This week we are finally sorting out her headstone. When she was first buried, we were told that it wasn't advisable to order for at least ten months. 'The ground needs to settle'. At the time it seemed like an eternity to wait, but fifteen months on, we still haven't arranged it, we've tried, but it's too distressing. It's too real.

Writing a short epitaph is harder than writing this book. How can we sum up 'Helen' in a few words. We can't. It's ridiculous. It's a physical confirmation of her death and I dread seeing it for the first time. Reality.

I'm sure that eventually we'll be pleased we had one erected. It will make putting flowers on her grave easier, and I know that when I die, my name will be added, and several feet below, I'll be back with my wife. As odd as it sounds, there is a very selfish comfort in that thought.

***

When Helen died, nobody could have imagined what 2020 had in store. It's never a good time to lose a loved one, but the Covid 19 pandemic has been a cruel and heartbreaking twist of fate for countless bereaved families.

I don't consider that we were lucky, but I'm thankful that Helen's final months were in a normal, if flawed world. It would have been unthinkable if she'd been unable to tick things off her wish list, unable to get treatment, unable to see the family. Shielding and yet still dying. It would have been a nightmare. A nightmare which many families have had to live through.

But I can't help thinking that if she hadn't developed cancer, we'd have been okay. We'd have been happy being with each other, despite the restrictions, we'd have been together. So yes, it would have been awful if she'd been ill this year, but selfishly, the reality is, I wish she was still here. We wouldn't have been lonely.

***

Before I met Helen, I always felt there was something missing in my life, she filled that gap. Now she's gone, that feeling is back, but the difference is, she left me with a much stronger foundation to build the rest of my life on. Having known her, I'm hopefully a better person, I have people who love me, and although it sometimes doesn't feel that way – she has left me with a reason to accept *my* 'new reality'. I have to be strong, because if nothing else, I owe her that.

***

In our original Wills, we both stated that we wanted to be cremated. So I was surprised when during her last few days, Helen told our son that she wanted to be buried.

It's wasn't something we'd discussed. We should have done. It was just taboo. Not a great conversation over a curry and a glass of wine!

When we visited the Cotswolds with Helen's cousin and school friend in May 2019, we spent a morning in Burford. It has a stunning church and a typical village graveyard. I remember saying how I experienced great peace in both church yards and cemeteries - and for some reason I found them a beautiful and calming place to visit.

I can't remember if Helen was privy to the conversation, (sadly I never will), but I do have some idea of how her mind worked, and it would come as no surprise to find that her decision to be buried, was unselfishly for my benefit.

She knew I would find grieving easier if I had a place to go – a place where she was sleeping. Somewhere I could talk to her, feel close to her and be totally myself. A refuge where I would be able to laugh, cry, confide and confess as if she was still sat beside me.

It is a comfort, and for whatever reason she had a change of heart. I'm pleased she did.

An uncharacteristically dark painting from Helen's university portfolio

GOING BACK

We have been friends with a lovely couple for several years who proved to be two of the most amazing human beings when our crisis began. During Helen's chemo treatment, (both times), Vi cooked meals for us most nights. She'd quietly leave them on our doorstep, so as not to disturb us and sent a message to say they were there.

They also own a static caravan in Hunstanton, again, every time Helen's treatment ended, they lent us the caravan, free of charge, so we that could get away and refocus our lives. It was a wonderful, kind and generous gesture. We had some lovely holidays in Norfolk – sometimes just the two of us, sometimes joined by friends. We couldn't thank them enough. Some acts of kindness will never be forgotten.

After Helen died, I was given the chance to return. It was only a few months since we'd been there together and it was always going to be a very different and difficult trip. But it felt good to be back. I played lots of guitar, I wrote songs, I walked along the beach. My daughter and grandson joined me for the last few days. We made new memories. On my second visit I wrote five thousand words of this book, including part of this chapter.

***

This is my second visit without her – last time was soon after she'd died and I needed to get away. Similarly, I felt the same urgency this time, the same need to get away.

But it wasn't that I wanted to escape from the people who love me, or from memories of Helen, in fact, it was quite the opposite. Being here alone, I feel I can evaluate how my life is moving on and changing, something which is nigh on impossible back home where everything is busily going on around me. A life which Helen is still an enormous part of – but also – she isn't.

It's strange. My last visit, I came armed with guitars and the need to write a song about our Hunstanton break earlier that year. Which I did. This time, I came equipped with my dad's old lap top and a compulsion to make inroads into writing this book.

I've been here three days, but only this afternoon did I take a guitar out of it's case. Which probably says more about me than I am prepared to accept. I don't make life easy for myself. I'm not very kind to me. I should be relaxing, chilling out and stepping back from normality, but no, I've challenged myself to write five thousand words before I head home. But that's me. As soon as I stop, I struggle. So I don't!

I wish that you were here to enjoy the walks along the beach, the basking in the autumn sunshine - the being with me. But you're not and begrudgingly I have to accept that.

You'd have enjoyed tonight's curry – I almost enjoyed it myself – but it's no fun eating alone – I just enjoy the cooking. Eating is just a means to an end.

I can picture the scenario. You'd have had your feet up on the chair, wrapped in one of your big woolly cardigans, drinking a glass of wine and watching TV whilst I cooked. Or you might be reading one of your books – you loved losing yourself in a biography or some sloppy romantic fiction!

Arguably, it wasn't earth shatteringly exciting, and with any one else it could well have been dull. But it wasn't with you. We'd laugh, talk, ignore the clock. It was perfect. We enjoyed our 'aloneness'. Now it's just 'loneliness'.

My trip to Hunstanton hasn't been my only return visit. I spent a few days at our friend's house in Dorset. We'd been their guests several times over the last couple of years. To go back, alone, was a bit odd for all of us, but because we have a lovely history together, we got through it. In the same way as going back to the caravan, it helped me realise that I still had a future. A very different future, and definitely not the one I'd have chosen, but I'm still very much alive.

It made me realise that I'm not facing a locked door. It's unlocked, and I just need to walk through it occasionally. My trips away brought that analogy into focus. I am still capable of having a laugh with friends, I don't need to feel ashamed if I enjoy myself. It's what she'd have wanted.

I'm very aware that I could easily become a boring widower, and it's important to me and Helen's memory that I don't let that happen. I haven't forgotten how to smile. My vacations to familiar places have helped. They've given my confused head the space to concentrate on how I need to move my life forward – on my own.

FACEBOOK POST 7th October 2019

Andy Smith is with **Helen Smith**.
7 October 2019 ·

Helen was far more private than me and rarely posted on facebook..
I've always worn my heart on my sleeve and my ramblings over the last few weeks have been so kindly received, welcomed and accepted.
Thanks to two amazing friends, I have had a lovely few days on the coast in a beautiful caravan, where i spent quite a bit of time alone - but also a couple of days with my daughter and grandson....very special and beautiful times.
I walked along the beach - the beach we walked - and I slept in the bed - the bed where we slept.
I went out for a meal on my own - and i went to the clubhouse on my own - i ticked boxes - and that is what life is all about at the moment - ticking boxes and surviving.
I played guitar and wrote songs that i never wanted to write - personal song - songs which show how much she meant to me - and hopefully are a testament to the wonderful life which we had together.
I hope she is looking down and feeling proud of me - but i suspect she is probably saying ...ANDREW SHUT UP!!

THINGS I MISS MOST

It's a dark Sunday afternoon and I'm feeling lonely. I've sorted out the house, I've done a load of washing, I've taken some fresh flowers to the cemetery. I'm feeling tired.

I found that old blanket, (the black and white stripy one), the one you used to lay under when you were feeling poorly. I climbed underneath it and I slept for over an hour. I needed to be close to something that had kept you warm. But really, it was your warmth that I longed to feel, your breath, your touch. I can't. I'm missing you.

I've never lived on my own. I lived with Mum and Dad until we got married - and then there was you. I've never been lonely in my life, but I am now – and I hate it.

Ironically, I now have time to do all those things I never had time to do, but instead, I waste hours by trying to do too much. My time management has gone to pot darling. I'm busy going round in circles most of the time.

I miss you being here. I miss watching you brush your hair, hearing you moving around the house. I miss hearing you sing and I miss your laughter. I even miss the unholy mess in your work room!

I miss your company, because you were my best friend. I miss talking to you. I loved how we sat and 'chunnered' for ages, but could also have the most comfortable silences. Now it's just silence.

I miss bringing your coffee and cereal every morning and I miss giving you a cuddle last thing at night. I miss running your bath, I miss cooking you a nice meal and I miss sharing a bottle of wine with you.

I miss going out and I miss staying in with you. I particularly hate Saturday nights. We loved our Saturday nights at home. Sometimes we'd go out, but given the choice, you'd prefer to 'slob out', have me cook a curry, and watch a load of junk on TV. Our favourite time of the week - I now dread.

So many times I think 'I must tell you that', or 'we must go there again', or 'you'd love this book'. I miss being able to share good news with you, I miss being able to tell you when I'm worried or scared. I could tell you - you understood. We understood each other. You made it better.

I miss being needed. I miss making phone calls for you, finding reference for your work, I miss scanning your artwork and sending off your invoices. I miss doing all those things that I did to help and protect you. I wish I could have protected you from the worst news of your life, but that was a bridge too far.

I miss being loved by you. My mum loves me, our kids love me, the grandchildren love me, my family love me, our friends love me - but it's not the same as our love.

Not only do I miss being loved by you, but I miss hearing you say it. We were always saying it. It was a promise we made in 1984 – a promise that we both kept.

***

I take some comfort from a memory of the morning you died. You were very weak. We knew that you were unlikely to see another sun go down. I'd told you a thousand times during the night, while you were sleeping, that I loved you. But in the dawn, I was able to tell you in one of your waking moments. You were too weak to say the words – but you mouthed them back 'Love you too'. It was our three squeezes. I will never forget..

Helen, there is no love like the love I had and still have for you. There never could be.....and I miss being able to tell you..

FACEBOOK PAGE 13th July 2020

Andy Smith
13 July ·

Another hour, another day, another week, another month..another year (nearly)....Time makes no difference.....I miss, I miss, I miss

US

So often it's those questions only Helen could answer. Something I can't remember, but I know she'd know. Something incredibly trivial, totally unimportant, but it becomes important, because she knows, and can't tell me.

I watch most of my TV on 'catch up' or 'box sets' – it works better for me that way. There was a recent series called 'Us' screened on BBC. It was based on a book by David Nichols.

I knew as soon as I started watching that Helen would have loved it – funny and sad in equal measure. Also, the story line was familiar - I'd read the book!

My problem was, I couldn't remember when I'd read it. If it had been during Helen's lifetime – she would definitely have indulged my recommendation, but if it had been in the last fifteen months – she'd have missed out.

It made me really sad. I would have enjoyed the series so much more if I'd known that we had a joint interest in the story. It's silly, but it's another of those unanswered questions. Not important – but of importance to me.

GUILT & REGRETS

Guilt can be, and frequently is, totally irrational. It creeps up on you in the middle of the night. It brings storm clouds on days which seemed to be going okay. It's destructive in the worst possible way. Guilt can overshadow all of the beautiful memories – and it shouldn't.

My dad could hardly walk in his final months, carers called twice a day, but they often weren't there at the times when they were most needed. It was a great strain on my ninety one year old mum.

Despite helping as much as we could, we weren't living under the same roof - we were very aware that she was struggling on a daily basis. Dad was also very conscious of the strain he was putting her under. I know that he felt guilty for being what he considered 'a burden', but what could he do? He would have been miserable in a nursing home – and there was no way my mum was going to let that happen!

She washed him, fed him, helped him when he fell. She pushed him around town in a wheelchair, she changed his sheets in the middle of the night when he was too weak to get out of bed. She honoured her vow of 'in sickness and in health' to the absolute and literal limit. She did everything for him – because she loved him – and because she wanted to.

But I had a very sad conversation with her the night of his death. She told me of her guilt. She worried that she 'might have lost patience with him a couple of times'...particularly on the second and third bout of changing bedclothes in the middle of the night.

I didn't tell her she was being ridiculous – I used kinder words. But it was ridiculous. She had been the most amazing, strong wife for not only his last twelve months, but for over sixty years of happy marriage. Yet at the point of loss, she dwelt on a desperate moment when she was tired and 'near her wits end'. At the time, I don't think I understood why it bothered her so much – but I do now.

Every one has their own guilt, often the guilt is for good reason. I know I was sometimes selfish, I know there were times when I took Helen for granted. I'm sure there were occasions when I didn't live up to expectations. But those times were hopefully few and far between. They shouldn't put a shadow over the thousands of days when we laughed, loved and wouldn't have wanted to be with anyone else.

Equally, I don't feel that I have a monopoly on this emotion. I'm sure there are friends or family who have a niggling guilt about something in their history with Helen, something that haunts their nights, something that they would sooner forget, but can't. The thing is, we aren't perfect, Helen wasn't perfect. Life would be very dull if we were. It's balancing the good things against the bad – and I'm pretty sure I know which way the scales will tip.

***

Guilt and regrets are two very different emotions. Guilt is usually about something done in the past, regrets are more likely to be something you didn't do, or should have done. They can also relate to the future. As long as someone is alive, you can change things. You can correct mistakes; you can massage your conscience. But once they are gone, everything is too late.

Wasted time is an enormous regret of mine, even if our lives didn't give us an option. We met late 1983 but we didn't marry until summer 1986.

I've read Helen's letters written over that three year period, and it's clear that we spent too much time apart. Often we wouldn't see each other for a fortnight – and then it would be a whirlwind forty eight hours and we'd be separated again.

The fact that we weathered such a difficult relationship for nearly three years is proof of our love, but it was hard. Helen was miserable a lot of the time. We both struggled.

Helen wanted to arrange our wedding for 1985, she'd have finished university and it wouldn't have been an issue. The problem was that we had no money. In fairness, we probably weren't any better off twelve months later when we finally did tie the knot.

Now I look back, and think that it was a wasted year. I regret that we didn't just throw caution to the wind and see where it blew us. Helen wanted to. I was the one who said we needed to 'save'.

Too often we were guilty of taking advice when we should have just been selfish, and done what *we* wanted to do. Times were very different back then. Hindsight is a wonderful thing. If only we could have banked those days apart and tagged them on to the end of her life....

***

The week that Helen was rushed into hospital, I'd had a stomach virus and had been sleeping in the spare room. *(The last thing she needed was to catch my germs.)* We slept apart for three nights, but it means that I can't remember the last night I went to bed with her – and that hurts. I still checked on her every few hours, but it wasn't the same. I regret that I wasn't there to hold her if she needed me. All I know is that our last night together was a monday....

This was one of my reasons for wanting her home the night before the funeral. We were able to sleep together once more, but sadly her sleep was going to last forever.

***

My biggest regret, *(which is also guilt),* is that Helen wasn't able to talk to me about dying. She didn't want to upset me. We talked about everything in our marriage, but a discussion about the most important thing in her life – we didn't. I know that she worried about how I'd cope when she was gone, but again, we didn't have 'that conversation' either. She wasn't worried about how I'd handle the everyday tasks, she knew I could cook, she'd taught me how to work the washing machine...no, it was how I'd manage without her there beside me that bothered her.

***

Since her death, I've discovered that Helen didn't confide in anybody about her mortality. Not her best friend, not her favourite cousin, not her children. She closed the curtains and it was off the agenda.

I wish she'd felt able to speak to someone. She wasn't being selfish. I'm pretty sure she felt that she was protecting us all, and trying to keep life as normal as possible. This worked when she was alive, but not after she'd gone.

I hate that she faced her destiny on her own, it seems a very lonely path, but then again, that is so far from the truth. Everyone around her loved her and supported her. We'd have moved mountains to keep her from harm. I'm sure the knowledge of how much we cared, was more than enough for her. Conversations about death weren't necessary, she wasn't alone and she knew it.

In all honesty, her reticence to talk should have come as no surprise. This was 'my Helen', the very quiet, private person, right to the end. I shouldn't feel guilt or regret, I should feel proud. I was just too much in love.

***

I regret all those things we can no longer do together. Places we can no longer visit together. People we can no longer see as a couple. There were so many things in our lives that we loved, which I will never do again. Some aren't physically possible without her - some would be just too painful.

We spent many happy times in Liverpool. It's one of my favourite cities. Our son spent four years at the university and we were frequent visitors. When Helen was planning her 'making memories' breaks, a trip to Liverpool was very high on the list. We had a wonderful time, but I will never go back. Every memory about the city involves Helen, and because they are such beautiful memories, a return visit could never be as good.

Helen was an amazing illustrator, but her speciality was her portrait painting. She loved drawing and painting faces. She was brilliant at capturing the personality of her subject, she always got the eyes right. Her paintings were like photos – but better!

Over the years, she painted or drew portraits of our children, our nieces and nephews, friend's children, pets and many private commissions. I know that since her death, these pictures have become even more special to those folk who still have them hanging on their walls.

Looking through the hundreds of books and magazines that she illustrated, it's easy to recognise the people she used as her models. They didn't need to be, but they are like 'fictional portraits', her eye for detail was incredible.

It was her intention to work on portraits of our grandchildren to give to our kids Christmas 2019. She took photos for reference, I found them on her phone. But she never had a chance to charge her paintbrush.....

She knew her time was finite, but I don't think she expected her end to be quite so sudden. She was planning to spend another Christmas with us, and she definitely intended to paint/draw the grandchildren.

After making so many people happy with portraits that she had lovingly painted over the years, it seems incredibly sad that she was deprived of the opportunity to leave us with such a personal memory. They would have been so treasured, and such a loving thing to do. Regretfully life is just too cruel at times.

FACEBOOK POST 15th December 2019

Andy Smith
15 December 2019 ·

When the person you love more than anything in the world is stolen – life begins a mix of a million emotions,
Was I there when you needed me?
Would I have done anything differently?
Did I say the right thing?
In truth, there are a million things I wish I had said, but there wasn't time...anyway, you probably didn't want to hear ...that was how you coped with the worst news imaginable, and that had to be your choice.. I just wish I'd been as strong as you...then we might have talked. We talked about everything...but not about you dying..I just wish we had.
There have been times when I have wondered if you loved me as much as I loved you – I've been told that's natural.....but today I found the card you sent for my 60th Birthday - nearly two years ago – it was so you – so full of love – so safe and happy in the life we had built together.....so content ...it made my cry...but it also brought me to my senses – and for some strange, peculiar reason – you did love me - unconditionally - and as you so frequently told me in your letters from nearly 40 years ago, and in your card from 2 years ago....you would love me forever...Well that's mutual xx

DENIAL

Denial is one of the major stages of grief. Probably one which I've mentioned more than any other over the last few chapters. It's been another way of coping.

Helen has been dead for over fifteen months, but I still expect to wake up in a morning and discover that the last year has been the world's worst and longest nightmare. The alarm's going to ring, and she'll be laid beside me, poking me in the back, telling me to go downstairs and get her coffee and cereal.

Part of me knows that I'm fooling myself, but the other side of my brain tells me that something so awful could never have happened.

I've written earlier about how when Helen was told in October 2018 that any treatment was palliative, denial was my automatic way of handling the awful news. It wasn't my choice. I didn't consciously decide that I wasn't going to accept it. I had no alternative. My brain made the decision for me.

Arguably, as a couple, it meant that I could still be 'me' with her. I wasn't breaking down in tears every five minutes and we could have a strangely normal life together. Obviously, things were different, but with my denial and Helen's reluctance to talk about her cancer, we managed pretty well. Whether it was right or wrong...who knows? But at the time, it worked for us.

I suppose that the downside of denial is that in the end, the truth comes out. Those are the times I dread. There are days when I'm very aware that Helen won't be watching 'Cash in the Attic' when I come home from work. I won't be calling her to say I've arrived at my gig, and then calling again to say that I'm on my way home. She won't be messaging me to tell me that we've run out of milk, or that her mum and dad can't get their TV to work. She will never phone me again just because she wants to tell me that she loves me and hear my voice. Those days are gone, and however much I want to believe the opposite, they are a part of my past, they will never happen again.

I don't think that Helen was in denial, she was frighteningly aware of the cancer that was ravaging her body, but she frequently told me that I was. Not in a judgemental way, but as a cautionary message. She worried how her death would impact on my life, and my refusal to accept the inevitable would ultimately cause me more pain. She was probably right.

***

My reluctance to accept that she is gone is a contradiction in itself – to me more than anyone. I can sit by her graveside, I can read her epitaph, but I still talk to her. I walk through the front door and say 'I'm home babe', because I always did. She will be the first person I speak to in the morning, and the last person I say goodnight to before I sleep....

The rational, unemotional side of me tells me that I'm acting like a fool. But I'm not rational, I'm very emotional, and I don't think I'm a fool!

Denial probably isn't right, but it's not wrong either. It's not as negative as guilt, and in a strange way it can be a comfort. More of a blanket than a reality...but a comfort. A blanket I sleep better under.

FACEBOOK POST 10th September 2019

'back to gigging'

Andy Smith
10 September 2019 ·

Today i got back in the saddle and did my first gig for a couple of months.
I knew it was going to be difficult - not just the gig - which was lovely - but all the routines I had...
The texting when i arrived, and then after the gig, phoning with a predicted 'arrive home' time, the walking through the front door to a pretty, smile on a beautiful but relieved face - the questions wanting to know how it had gone...her telling me about her day...

Next time - thursday - will hopefully be a bit easier and each time, a bit less painful.
I will always remember those times which I took so easily for granted - and will always long for them once again.
I would have treasured them so much more if I'd known they were going to end.

Helen in the saddle - looking far better than I ever could!

FOUR LETTER WORD

Bob Dylan wrote a song back in the 1960's, (*showing my age*) called 'Love is Just a Four Letter Word'. The phrase, like so many of his titles has manifested itself into our language. But it's so true. Love can be the reason for both the best and the worst days of your life. 'The greater the love, the greater the loss' is a maxim I have frequently been quoted over the last few months. But I wouldn't have loved less to grieve less – even if it had been a possibility.

When I fell in love with Helen, it was as close to 'love at first sight' as you could get – and it was the same for her. Neither of us were prepared, or expected to be hit by such an enormous thunderbolt. It took us both by surprise. Actually, it was pretty inconvenient! We had no money, she was a student. We lived over a hundred miles apart. We didn't own a car....

Why couldn't we have fallen in love with someone who had a 'proper job' and lived in the same town?

Maybe just fate...

Four months before meeting Helen, I'd been on holiday to St Ives in Cornwall. The day I headed home, unbeknown to me, she arrived, checked into the same hotel, and had a weeks holiday with her cousin and brother. We missed each other by a few hours. What are the chances?

But in the August of 1983, the 'big romance' might not have happened. I had a steady girlfriend, Helen wasn't in a serious relationship, but there was no shortage of interested suitors – I expect she was enjoying the freedom of being single and popular.

I like to think that if our holidays had coincided, we might still have ended up together, but it would have been less likely. The fact that we were fortunate enough to get a second chance four months later proved that the planets were finally in line and things were meant to be - Fate.

Our love never faltered. It changed. The fireworks can't last forever. Sometimes it was pushed to the limit, but ultimately, it matured into something far more beautiful. Not only did we have an incredible love – but we were best friends. The ultimate recipe for a good marriage.

The loss was always going to be enormous. I knew it would be. After her diagnosis, I tried to picture *'a life'* without Helen being the most important part of it. I couldn't. I went into denial, an understandable and natural defense mechanism. Unfortunately, when the time came and she died, I was totally unprepared for the tsunami, not just for me, but for everyone around us.

***

The wonderful thing about love is that there are so many different types. When our children were born, we developed a new love - an unconditional love. We wanted to protect our beautiful, tiny, little people from everything horrible in the world - forever!

As new parents, particularly with our first born, we seemed to spend the first few months in a state of total panic. Has he got a temperature? Shouldn't he be sitting-up by now? Why won't he go to sleep? Is he deaf? Is he blind? Why doesn't he smile more? Is he happy? Does he love us? I'm sure we weren't the first parents to feel that way.

By the time our daughter came along, there was still that same unconditional love and need to protect, but there wasn't such blind panic all of the time. Hopefully we had improved as parents!

They went to school and university, found jobs. We were so proud of both of them. We never stopped worrying about them, but they were genuine people and they were leading good lives. They had friends, hobbies and a strong sense of right. Within a year of each other, they both married. We loved their partners and life was almost complete.

At the start and the end of December 2017, both couples gifted us with our first two grandchildren. Life *was* now complete. I don't think I'd ever seen Helen so happy. She was a natural nanna. She was there to help both families whenever she could, and that unconditional love was back for a new generation.

I used to joke that they loved her more than they loved me...and she would say that they loved me more than they loved her. They loved us both.

(She would also say that I loved them more than I loved her. But she knew that wasn't true!)

***

Helen had already had a course of successful chemotherapy in 2016. The cancer had been caught early and there was every hope that it was gone for good. She had regular scans and blood tests and although the 'result appointments' were a worry, they were always 'clear', until her visit in October 2018.

We were getting on with our lives. Everything was good. Our children were happy and settled. Our grandchildren were close by and an enormous part of our every day existence. Helen was busy with her illustration work. I had a diary full of gigs. We had amazing friends. We were very contented - and BANG!

More chemotherapy was prescribed. But after three months with horrible side effects, the treatment had very little effect. There was an option for more – but it had made her feel so ill, she decided that she needed a break, and didn't want to go through it again – which rightly or wrongly had to be her decision.

It was suggested that she might be eligible for a drug

trial. Ironically, apart from having terminal cancer, she was very healthy. She was a perfect candidate for an experimental test. That was her new mission!

Unfortunately, there was a strict regime of examinations, invasive biopsies, eligibility checks, frequent trips to London. Four months later, when due to start the trial, her health had deteriorated to such an extent, that it was decided she wasn't strong enough to face it. I felt so sad for her. All the doors had been slammed in her face. The drug trial was the last card in her hand. There were no other options.

***

When we were told that the person I planned to grow old and grey with was on borrowed time – it was like being hit by a train. Our children were devastated. We couldn't protect them from this. There were tears and hugs, encouraging words about fighting it. But we all knew that we were just fooling ourselves.

Helen worried about me, as did my children. I worried about Helen and the kids. They worried about her. We all worried about each other. Our family became incredibly tight, even tighter than before. There was a lot of love.

Our children had been protected from death. I don't know why, it just turned out that way. Their first experience of losing someone really close was with the death of their grandad, my dad. By that time they were both in their mid twenties.

I was nine when my own grandad died – and I can still

remember the days leading up to it. But I was shielded by my childhood and although it's in my memory – it's a bit of a blur. I just remember how much I loved him. It was something far more tangible for my children, but dad was ninety one and had been poorly for a while. It was awful, but it wasn't a shock.

The four days up to Helen passing away, my son, daughter and me spent virtually every moment by her bedside. Despite, or because of the tragic situation we were all living through, I felt the enormous strength and bond of our family love. It was our cement.

I talked to both my son and my daughter about what they believed would happen to their mum once she died. My son is a Christian, my daughter doesn't believe in God. I took great heart in that they both, with their religious belief and lack of belief, held the same view. They felt that one day they would be reunited with her. One believing, because of what the bible said, and the other because they believed there could be an afterlife without a biblical justification. I didn't know what to think, but I was pleased to know that they didn't think that this was the final chapter.

To be in the presence of someone's final moments is almost spiritual. I suppose it's an honour and a privilege. Helen had been given a host of drugs to ease the pain and we were told that she wouldn't wake up again, she would quietly drift away – which she did. Her final forty five minutes were very peaceful. To know that she was no longer suffering was our main concern, but when she took her final breath, the world we knew died with her.

Suddenly, the diagnosis, the months of treatment, the endless hours spent in chemotherapy bays, the disappointments, the unanswered prayers, the pain - they all rolled into one and turned black. My daughter fell to the floor, my son was in tears, my wife and their mum was dead.

I hope that at this point, at that precise moment in time, I was a good dad. I needed to be. This was my time to be strong for them. But there was no script. I'd been at my dad's side when he died, I recognised the signs of life slipping away, but this wasn't the same. Our children had never been witness to anything so heartbreaking in their lives. I felt guilt that they had to watch their mum die, but I was also glad that they were there. In years to come, I hope that they will take comfort from the fact that she was there for the start of their lives – and they were beside her at the end of hers - and she was never alone, and she was always loved.

Their grief is different to mine. Their love is different. Something I need to appreciate and understand. We created these two people. They had loved their mum for the whole of their lives, she'd always been there. They didn’t know a life without her. They loved her with a passion and suddenly she was gone.

I have often wished that I’d died and Helen had survived.

Not because they love me less, but because she is needed more. When they were younger, and even towards the end, they were far more likely to tell Helen their problems than me. She was an incredible 'listener'. She would never judge, she would be kind. She wouldn't tell them what to do, but far more likely would tell them what *she would d0* - and then let them decide.

I'm sure that both of our children's partners would also agree that Helen was never like a 'mother-in-law'. She was more like a 'second' mum, and they both loved her as a person and friend as well as the parent of their partner.

A child's loss is enormous, whatever their age, they have their whole lives stretching out before them. But like mine, there will always be someone missing. When new grandchildren are announced and born, however happy we may be, there's bound to be a tinge of sadness that a very proud nanna can't be part of the proceedings. I like to think that she'll be watching. I hope so.

***

When someone dies, particularly someone who is still quite young, the ripples spread wide. It's very easy when you're at the centre of the storm to forget that there is a host of other people grieving and missing the person you loved. Someone they loved too.

Both Helen and me came from two very close families. She left a brother, an older sister, her mum and dad, numerous aunts, uncles, cousins, nieces, nephews. There was a similar list on my side of the family.

Her cousin was always one of her best friends. When she heard that Helen was only expected to last a few days, she arrived at the hospital in Coventry, from The Wirral, virtually unannounced. Helen had been in hospital for nearly a fortnight and she'd been adamant that the only visitors she wanted to see were the children and me. It was a worry. But when her cousin arrived, she was visibly pleased to see her, and from thereon in, she started receiving visitors. It was an enormous relief. It might seem selfish, but people needed the opportunity to say goodbye.

***

It's said, 'You can choose your friends...'

We have an enormous network of friends. I suppose because our lives were quite varied, they came from all walks of life. There were old school friends, university friends, my friends, her friends, holiday friends, those made in the school playground when the kids were small, musicians, artists....

When Helen moved to Rugby, she needed to meet new people. I hoped it wouldn't be a problem. She worked from home, she was painfully shy, and there wasn't going to be a lot of chance. I didn't want her to be lonely or homesick. It was very important to me that she was happy and settled in her new life.

I needn't have worried. Because Helen was the person she was, everyone she met wanted to be her best friend. I used to tell her that our flourishing social calendar was

only because people loved her so much – she was the attraction – and they weren't really interested in me, I was the hanger on!
Since her death – I have been proved wrong.

For the seven months before 'Lockdown', I was rarely home in an evening. Virtually every night, I would be invited to either friends or family for something to eat. I used to call them my 'widower meals'!

I would be dragged out for a drink by mates. I had a constant stream of visitors. My phone never stopped ringing. It was as if someone had put a timetable together to keep me busy. They hadn't of course. Why were they doing it? Because they loved Helen, and they were looking after me – for her.

***

Helen was a very private person. She chose her friends carefully. But if you were her friend – she loved you and she would be there for you 'come what may', even when all hell was breaking loose in her own life.

It was all about 'the person' in Helen's book. Her friends are a bit like a reflection of her. Invariably they are kind, happy, positive people. Helen's glass was always half full - never half empty. Her friends are similar.

She loved them all, but there were a few very special people in her life. Her cousin, her old school friend, the friend who took her to chemo when I couldn't and the friend she told she wanted by her side when she died. (*In the end, that wasn't possible, but it shows the strength of love that she felt for her mate who'd travelled all the way from Dorset, desperate for the chance to say one last goodbye.)*

It's easy to underestimate a friend's grief. Being at the centre of the storm, my grief is twenty four seven, a friend's grief is different. Life has to go on. A friend can't take a few days off work to 'be sad'. They aren't expected to suddenly burst into tears in the supermarket, *(even though they might).* There probably won't be the same love and understanding from people 'outside of the circle'. Normal routine needs to continue, and that makes it incredibly hard.

When I had counselling, I was taught to recognise the 'triggers' that would result in my worse moments. It works. They are still awful, but you can prepare for them. This is probably one of the reasons why friends find it so hard, its being totally unprepared for those overpoweringly, desperate times.

Something totally random can be the catalyst for a total meltdown. A song on the radio, a photograph, a letter, a memory suddenly slipping in from your subconscious. A dream with your friend in it, an echo. Strangely, depending on your mood, these things can bring joy and laughter, but invariably they bring tears.

I'm in no position to give advice, it's not what this book is about, but talking to someone who knew your friend helps. Personally, I find it easier to give comfort than be the recipient of it.

So yes. Love is a four letter word. But it was always of paramount importance in our marriage and our lives together. Love is the cause of my pain – but it will also be my greatest comfort and strength.

If love was a cure for cancer, Helen would still be with us.

FACEBOOK POST 2nd February 2020

> **Andy Smith** is with **Helen Smith**.
> 2 February ·
>
> Another month has passed – another month without my best friend – and tomorrow it will be 6 months since she left us.
> Last month, Helen's Mum and my dear Mother-in-Law, also passed away. I like to think they are reunited.
> It doesn't get any easier living without Helen, in fact in many ways it's much harder...the need to accept that she has gone and I'm not going to wake up and find her sleeping by my side are a painful reminder of how fragile life can be.
> Tonight I've been watching the videos of Helen in Liverpool last April – dancing the night away at The Cavern..she looks so full of life..and happy...which she was....surrounded by special friends.
> Then I watched the videos of a very different Helen. The Nanna. The 'Family' Helen - reading stories to the babies, making them giggle. Feeling so much love it almost overwhelmed her....a very caring and loving Helen.
> I take comfort in the fact that Helen both loved and was loved in equal measure. Something you can't buy., something you aren't entitled to...but something you earn by being a special, giving person....and she was.
> I adored everything about her and I miss having her by my side and i always will x

MYSTERY

SWANSONG

When Helen was fighting her way through her first bout of chemotherapy in 2016, she would often disappear to bed early. The tiredness, the nausea and the handful of drugs made sleep an easy option. I would usually stay downstairs and watch TV.

One evening I decided to watch 'Once'. It's a musical, but not in the conventional style. For the most part, the songs are accompanied on acoustic guitar or piano. It's set in Dublin and is a beautiful film. When it ended, I decided I was going to write a musical, especially for Helen - and I did.

After two years of working with an amazing woman and her equally amazing theatre company, a scriptwriter (who took my story, rewrote it for stage – and made it very funny), an incredible cast, a young and gifted pianist - it all started coming together, and in July 2019 we had four sell out shows at a small theatre in the centre of Birmingham.

The venture took up a lot of my time. Time when Helen was ill. But she always encouraged me to go to the rehearsals, to see the guys, to have some fun. She knew that it was a safety valve for me, not an escape – I didn't need to escape, but it gave me some 'head space', which I probably did need.

Two weeks before the premiere, Helen started deteriorating fast. There were London hospital appointments several days a week, blood tests, transfusions. Things weren't looking good. I decided I had no choice but to 'step back' and abandon ship. Helen was always going to be my main priority.

Our show was left without a guitarist and a composer. I remember having a conversation with several members of the team and telling them my decision. Despite the mountain they had to climb, they showed a love and kindness which really moved me. They wouldn't have allowed me to carry on even if I'd wanted to.

Suddenly the show became so much more important to all of the cast and the people involved. Now they were doing it for her. Helen *was* the heart of 'Snowfall in July'..

She didn't want me to walk away from it. She felt guilty. This had been my project for the last three years and she'd *'be fine'*, she wanted me to have my moment. But my mind was made up. I hate letting people down, but I knew it was the right thing to do. My heart, my head and all my new theatre friends agreed with me.

I went to Opening Night on my own. I didn't have a clue what to expect. I didn't know how the stage was going to be set, I hadn't heard some of the actors singing my songs. I didn't want to sit on my own, *(which I didn't)*. It was very scary.

The show was brilliant. I have a message on my mobile, sent to Helen on my train journey home, I sound so happy that it was a success. The following morning, Helen announced that I needed to lay my hands on a wheelchair, because she was coming on Closing Night.

***

Lots of our friends had bought tickets for both the Saturday Matinee and also the evening performance. We pushed Helen, in her wheelchair through the busy streets of Birmingham. We met mates and family coming out of the afternoon performance, and we joined those going to the 7.30 show. It was a lovely fun event, even before it started!

The Director led Helen and me into the theatre ahead of the audience and sat us in the best seats. The show began, she laughed, she cried, she squeezed my hand. She was so proud, her eyes were alive with excitement.

After saying a quick 'Hello/Goodbye' to some of the cast, we wheeled her back through the drunken streets of Birmingham, and waved goodbye to our holiday friends who were standing on the platform at New Street Station. They knew they wouldn't see her again. This was the last goodbye. She smiled and played it down – like only Helen could.

We didn't know at the time, but it was her last night out. Six days later she was rushed into hospital, and three weeks after holding my hand in a tiny little theatre in Birmingham – she made her final exit.

That summer's evening in July 2019 has become one of the many defining moments of our marriage. Helen was in an awful lot of pain, she was tired, she was taking loads of drugs, but she was adamant that she was going to see the show. She was making a statement. She was there beside me because she loved me. She was there because the thirty six years we'd known and adored each other were as precious to her as they were to me. Nothing had really changed since Boxing Day 1983 - and if I ever doubted that our feelings were equal – she proved it that night.

NEVER APART

a song from Snowfall in July
(written for Helen, Valentines Day 2017)

You are to me – the light of the morning.
You were my first love – and you'll be my last.
You're my beginning and end,
You are the truth that won't bend.
With the last beat of my heart
Say you will be, always with me,
Never Apart

I won't be scared – if you're here beside me
No one can harm us – providing you're near.
We are the ink that won't fade.
We are the vows that we made,
With the last beat of my heart
Say you will be, always with me
Never Apart

LOOKING FORWARD

As I've compiled the chapters of this book, *(written in the five months subsequent to the anniversary of her death),* I've realised the many contradictions in my writing - and my life. Sometimes I'm positive, often I want to join her. Sometimes I'm coping pretty well, other times I'm writing because I need to express my pain. But that's how it is!

I could edit and make it flow, but that would be a compromise and ruin the integrity of the book – and I'm not prepared to do that. The fact is, I've been brutally honest, life without her doesn't make sense, it doesn't flow, it's as unpredictable as a local bus service.

I can go through a dozen mood changes within a sixty minute window. I can laugh and cry in the same breath. I can be lonely and long for solitude at the same time. This is me, this is my grief. A year down the line, it's still raw and it's still overwhelming.

I can only say how I feel, or how I've felt at any given time. But I know I'm not alone. This can be a version of anybody's story that has lost someone special. The only difference is the landscape and how you see it.

My journey falls well short of perfect, it's been a bumpy ride, but it's been 'my journey', I feel no need to apologise or justify. I've made some big mistakes, I've been cruel to myself, I've blamed everyone, living and heavenly, but the truth is no-one's to blame. Not even me. Life is just a 'roll of the dice', trying to get your head round that is the difficult part. Nothing we could have done would have changed the outcome.

It's the total randomness of mortality which is the stumbling block. If I'd known when I first met Helen back in 1983 that she would die at fifty six years old, would I have done anything differently? Yes, I'd have done loads of things differently, but then it wouldn't have been the life we had – a life that was imperfect but beautiful. The randomness and the 'not knowing' is probably how it needs to be – however hard that is when the nightmare begins.

Helen bequeathed us a world which was a better place because of her existence - and that is something worth clinging on to. I still feel anxiety, guilt and desperation at some point most days of the week. It's exhausting. But I don't want to lose her. Helen was the biggest part of my life when she was alive, in a million ways, she still is – I don't want that to change. Better the pain than the anaesthetic I suppose.

***

I still look after my grandson every Monday. Ironically, I spend more time with him than any other human being in my life and I adore every bone in his thirty four month old body.

I knew when I woke yesterday morning that I was going to struggle with the day – I was feeling lonely. Helen wasn't close. But I was pleased to have the distraction of my little friend.

Halfway through the day, we hit a wall. He was tired and I probably wasn't being as much fun as usual. I raised my voice to him – something I never do. He was broken-hearted and just hugged me. He knew that he'd overstepped the mark, he didn't know why, but he knew he had. I told him that Grandad was sorry, but he was 'very sad today, and that he was really missing Nanna'. He put his arms around my neck and through his tears said, 'But you've got me Grandad'.

And that is the bottom line. I have him. I have our beautiful grandaughter, I have our children, our family, our friends. I no longer have Helen, but I have a thousand connections with her. I might feel lonely, but I'm not alone.

Tomorrow, next week, a year down the line, I don't expect to feel that much different, I'm still going to miss her. Life will still ring hollow. The house will still be too quiet. The bed will still feel cold and empty. But I'm lucky, because I'm young enough to have a future. Not the one I'd have chosen, but the years ahead mustn't be wasted.

I can hear Helen saying 'Get over it', in the same tone of voice as when a few days before she died, she told me to 'Find someone new, preferably someone rich!' I won't – on either count – and she knew I wouldn't.

***

At the start of this book, I mentioned that Helen was frequently a part of my dreams. She still is, but they've changed.

Now in my dreamworld, I have a strong sense that she's leaving me, she's more detached. It's like meeting an old girlfriend and realising that you're still in love with them, but they've moved on, and you haven't.

She's wearing the same clothes, she's the same person, our lives are still intertwined, but there's a void separating us, a void I can't comprehend. She's slowly slipping away and I can do nothing about it. I want my dreams to be like our life was – but increasingly, they're not. I wake up sad.

I suppose it's my sub conscience telling me that life has to change. We will always love each other, but there's an ever widening gap between the past and the present. A present, which however good – won't be *as good*, and a past which will never be forgotten, and always longed for.

I'm very fortunate, I have an incredible network around me, and I'm very aware that there are those who don't have that luxury. I'm frequently reminded that it's still 'early days'. We had thirty six wonderful years together and we've only been apart for fifteen months. It's hardly surprising that I still feel like I'm on the same page as the day she died.....

But pages have turned, because things change in tiny ways. I can now laugh at the funny lines in her letters, the lines that used to make me cry. I can look at her photographs and think how lucky I was – and not how unlucky I am, (*not always, but sometimes*). I can watch programmes on TV that we used to enjoy together and not start throwing things around the room and shouting at 'The Almighty'!

I loved and was loved more than most people could ever dream of. I should be more grateful. I have a thousand regrets – I'm human – we don't always get it right. But I also have a million beautiful memories.

If she's watching over me, I hope she understands why I wrote this book, and I hope that she's quietly proud. If I was able to ask her whether she thought it was a good idea, and did she mind? Well, I can picture her rolling her eyes, smiling and telling me to 'Get on with it', because like so many times in our marriage, if it was something I wanted to do, she'd have let me do it. I know she wouldn't have done the same thing, but I'm sure she would have done something to honour the most precious years of her life. Probably a painting.

There will always be an enormous emptiness, but she deserves better than a miserable, wallowing widower. She would understand how hard it's been and hate that she has caused such agony, (*even if it's through no fault of her own*). But she would want me to get on with my life – see a future in a world without her, enjoy the positives and try to overcome the negatives. That's my kick up the bum!

At the end of the day, Helen was the kindest and most beautiful person I've ever met. If she was here, she'd cry with me, hold me close, kiss me on the forehead and make it all okay. Because that's what Helen did.
That is one of the million reasons why I loved her, and will never forget her.

FACEBOOK POST 24th August 2020
positive end

Andy Smith
24 August ·

I've been reading a really good book on grief - maybe not the lightest of reading - but it has been immensely helpful and a fitting extension to the counselling I received from Myton Hospice.
It's good to know that the way I feel is not wrong, strange or self indulgent...
But my grief is 'unique'....
Nobody has felt the way I do.
If I had died first, Helen's grief would have been different....even though we were like the same person in a million ways!
I didn't meet Helen until I was 25 years old, and I was 61 when she died. So hopefully, I might, if lucky(?) have another 25 years....and so if I wrote a book about loss, my analogy would be a sandwich!!
The best bit is always going to be the bit in the middle, but the bread can be surprisingly nice too - you just need to taste it...and not leave it at the side of the plate.
It might sound daft - but it's a new road to walk down x